Solid Foundation Sermon Starters

# PASTORAL EPISTLES

*Blueprints for 28 messages
built upon God's Word*

D1314325

## Wayne E. Shaw

STANDARD
PUBLISHING

Cincinnati, Ohio

# Dedication

**Those Whom I Have Taught to Preach**

Who preach
Who teach preaching
Who love to hear the Word of God

**Those Who Have Taught Me to Preach**

In memory of Earl C. Hargrove, Enos E. Dowling, James S. Stewart
Members of the Academy of Homiletics

**Those Who Have Taught Preaching With Me**

Homileticians—John Webb, Chuck Sackett, J. K. Jones
Cohorts—James Strauss, Robert Lowery, Paul Boatman, Gary Hall, Tom Ewald,
Bruce Parmenter

**Those Who Have Made My Teaching of Preaching Possible**

My wife and partner—Janet
My sons—Haydn, Scott, Barton, Errett
My colleagues at Lincoln Christian College and Seminary

All Scripture quotations, unless otherwise indicated, are taken from the HOLY BIBLE, NEW INTERNATIONAL VERSION®. NIV®. Copyright © 1973, 1978, 1984 by International Bible Society. Used by permission of Zondervan Publishing House. All rights reserved.

Cover design by Grannan Graphic Design LTD

Interior design by Robert E. Korth

Edited by Jim Eichenberger
© 1999 by The Standard Publishing Company
All rights reserved.
Printed in the U.S.A.

Solid Foundation is an imprint from
The Standard Publishing Company, Cincinnati, Ohio.
A division of Standex International Corporation.
06 05 04 03 02 01 00 99                    5 4 3 2 1

# Contents

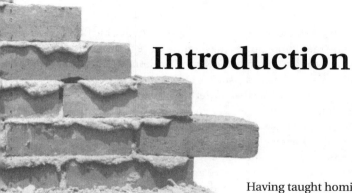

# Introduction

Having taught homiletics for a third of a century, I feel the need to state my opinion about the proper and improper uses of borrowed sermon outlines. If misused, they have their severe downside. There is no substitute for brooding over the Biblical text to find its meaning, relating it to the needs of the hearers, and communicating it with clarity, sparkle, and passion. But the preacher is rare indeed who has never borrowed another preacher's outline to develop a sermon topic or text. Hence the value of books like this.

## I. FOR PREACHERS

### A. Chapter sermons

Chapter sermons on each of the Pastoral letters (including the overview sermon and the four "book" sermons) illustrate one approach to preaching through larger sections of Scripture. They aim at the time-honored goal of applying the message of longer passages to our situation.

### B. Advantage of using longer Scriptures

The advantage of preaching from longer passages is that it helps us to look at the forest as well as the trees, and it often keeps us from violating the authenticity of the text. Its disadvantage is that we cannot examine the unique texture of any tree in detail.

### C. Cautions

Planning to preach a series of expository sermons carries with it necessary cautions: Be careful not to lecture on a Bible book, do not preach in the past tense, and do not dump unstructured exegetical ideas wholesale on the congregation.

### D. The proper use of borrowed sermon outlines

1. Sermon outlines can serve as **"structural models"** for other preachers and teachers.

   Aside from the gracious gift of God, there are three time-tested ways of learning to preach: homiletical principles, practice, and models. Good models show us concrete ways to structure a sermon in a rich variety of forms.

2. Sermon outlines can be **"pump primers"** for preachers and teachers.

We do not need help when ideas are hot and the sermon outline flows. We may need to prime the pump, however, when we have researched the text thoroughly and prayed and pondered over the sermon without awakening the muse within us. Sometimes a start is all we need to get the sermon flowing, and sometimes we need an orderly, precise way of structuring what we want so much to say.

3. Sermon outlines can be **"road maps"** for both the hearers and the preacher.

Studies have shown that hearers listen better and stay more engaged when the sermon outline and transitions between ideas are clear. One way of adding interest to a sermon is to have an interesting outline. Main headings act like the headlines and subheadings in a newspaper to highlight the big ideas. A clear outline also helps the preacher to stick to the main road and to arrive at his destination without wandering and roaming about.

4. Sermon outlines can provide the **"skeletons"** to structure important ideas and applications.

Many of the major metaphors in the New Testament emphasize by their nature how important good structure is: (1) anatomy—the church as the body of Christ; (2) agriculture—the structure of seedtime and harvest in many of the parables of the Kingdom of God; (3) athletics—the Christian life as a race according to the rules; (4) army—rules of discipline and training for Christian warfare; (5) architecture—building the church on the proper foundation with Christ as the chief cornerstone.

Sometimes the structure needs to stand out clear and clean like the walls of a skyscraper. At other times structure needs to serve the sermon ideas beneath the surface like the skeleton in our bodies. Without a deliberate skeletal structure, our sermon would be a gelatinous blob dumped out on the congregation.

## E. The improper use of borrowed sermon outlines

1. A sermon outline is not a sermon. Without supporting materials and application, an outline is merely a lifeless skeleton without flesh and blood. To rely too heavily on the outline, therefore, is to turn the sermon into an abstract and lifeless discourse without impact.

2. A borrowed outline is not to be preached "as is." It is designed to stimulate your sermon preparation. It is meant to be the alpha not the omega of sermon construction.

3. A borrowed outline is not to be a short cut to replace in-depth Bible study, fervent prayer, effective supporting material, and careful application.

4. A borrowed outline ought not stifle our growing ability to structure our own sermons. It should not dam up the stream of creativity in our lives.

5. Borrowed outlines need to be carefully evaluated theologically, logically, and psychologically. Sometimes they are more cute than convicting.

6. A borrowed outline is only one preacher's approach to expounding and applying the Word of God. It is certainly not the only way, and may not be the best way, to structure a sermon on a particular topic or text.

7. Growing congregations demand that sermons be interesting and few sermon outlines by themselves are inherently interesting. It takes careful treatment of Scripture, effective use of supporting materials, and astute application to produce a compelling sermon.

   Borrowed sermon outlines can be assets or liabilities depending on how we use them.

## II. FOR STUDENTS OF PREACHING

### A. Sermon models

Across the centuries students have studied sermon models as an important component in learning to preach. The approaches included here were designed to illustrate a variety of sermon patterns while remaining true to the Biblical text. The goal of studying sermon models is not to become preoccupied with clever creative forms, but rather to find the best vehicle for transporting Biblical content and impact.

### B. Sermon strategies and patterns

1. "Christ: The Heart of It All" (page 9) introduces the other sermons but with the lens focused on Christ in the development of each heading.
2. "A Church That Pleases God" (page 11) highlights three key concepts in the Pastorals and draws them together climactically in Christ.
3. "The Saga of a City Church" ( page 61) focuses on Ephesus as the urban context for 1 and 2 Timothy.
4. "Leading the Charge" (page 13) moves from problem to solution in each of the headings in order to sustain the attention and make application to the person in the pew.
5. "The Healthy Church" (page 15) recognizes the "thanksgiving" section of the letter as a literary device that Paul often used to compress the important themes into a capsule containing the major theme of the book. Also, along with "Praise God!" (page 51), it attempts to preach "doxologically" in order to encourage praise and to offer it through the sermon.
6. "The Last Letter From My Father" (page 29) is a narrative sermon designed to capture both an important theme of the letter and the emotional dynamics between Paul and Timothy. It especially targets business people in the congregation.
7. "Being a Strong Disciple" (page 33) utilizes images in the text to "embody" its meaning and to apply it. To discover the meaning of the text and to stimulate one's own imagination for developing the sermon, one should always look at the images in the text.
8. "Triumph in Troubled Times" (page 35) uses a problem-solution inductive approach. It illustrates that the "newer forms" can gain and hold attention as they unfold the Biblical text.
9. "God's Photo Album" (pages 53, 55) is a two-sermon series that uses several Bible characters mentioned in 2 Timothy to focus on the meaning of servant leadership.
10. "Friends or Foes?" (page 57) uses two antithetical headings to emphasize

one theme: how we treat the gospel determines whether we are God's friend or foe.

### C. Suggestions for further sermon series

1. Many of these outlines could become sermon series in themselves, allowing the preacher to treat preaching values in the text more thoroughly.
2. Each of the main headings in "Christ: The Heart of It All" could be developed into a helpful series because each is an important theme in the Pastorals.
3. "Leading the Charge" could be the lead sermon in a series that expands each of the main headings into a sermon that treats each Biblical text in greater detail.
4. Most of the chapter sermons could be expanded into a series. Each sermon, for example, in 1 Timothy could be expanded into a worthwhile series, either by developing each main heading into an individual sermon or by combining some of the main headings and expanding others.
5. Healthy relationships and attitudes are essential for healthy churches. "Practice Healthy Relationships" (page 25) could become the basis for four sermons about how to treat different groups in the church. "Exhibit a Healthy Attitude" (page 27) could be expanded to four sermons about areas in which a Christ-like attitude is so important.

The possibilities are nearly endless for the preacher who has a vivid imagination, is a thorough student of the Word, and has a keen insight into the needs of people. Paul Scherer once said that the only thing that will ever replace preaching is better preaching. May the study of these sermon outlines help you to preach better.

## III. FOR FURTHER STUDY

The serious servant of God will want to go deeper into the Word than one small volume of sermon outlines can take him. I suggest that those desiring more background in these three letters refer to the following volumes.

Barclay, William. *The Letters to Timothy, Titus and Philemon*. Edinburgh: The Saint Andrew Press, 1960. (Though older and somewhat dated, the commentary is valuable for background, word studies, and application.)

Knight III, George W. *Commentary on the Pastoral Epistles. A Commentary on the Greek Text*. Grand Rapids: William B. Eerdmans Pub. Co., 1992. (For those who want to dig deeper into the Greek text of the New Testament.)

Stott, John R. W. *Guard the Truth: The Message of I Timothy and Titus*. Downers Grove: Inter-Varsity Press, 1996. (A first-rate Biblical expositor who does not shun the hard work of dealing with the text and treating alternative interpretations clearly and fairly. He does tend to slant his interpretations of church order as "office" over "function".)

_____. *The Message of II Timothy: Guard the Gospel*. Downers Grove: Inter-Varsity Press, 1973.

Towner, Philip H. *I and II Timothy and Titus*. Downers Grove: Inter-Varsity Press, 1994. (Briefer treatment by a first-rate teacher with mission experience and perspective on the Pastorals.)

# Christ: The Heart of It All
## (Christ in the Pastorals)

### *1 & 2 Timothy; Titus*

I was asked to be president of the 1999 North American Christian Convention (NACC), a yearly gathering of members of the Christian Churches/Churches of Christ. One of my first responsibilities in that capacity was to develop a convention theme.

Two events led me to that theme. The first was my open-heart surgery in June 1997, that replaced my aortic valve with an artificial one. I discovered 148 references in the New Testament, and over 800 references in the Old Testament to the heart, 400 of them referring to the mind. To be a Christian, therefore, is to commit one's whole inner being to Christ, including one's mind, will, emotions, and conscience.

The other event occurred in one of my preaching classes as we listened to a recording of "The Rending of the Veil" by James S. Stewart. It struck me why he has so influenced my preaching and my faith. The center of his message is always the Christ.

Hence, "Christ: The Heart of It All," became the theme of that convention. Christ is also the heart of the Pastorals. He is only a few words away from anything else Paul wrote in his letters to Timothy and Titus. He is our hope; our Savior; our enabler; our source of grace, mercy, and peace; our resurrected Lord; our mediator between God and us; our ransom for our sins; our sovereign King; our King of kings and Lord of lords; our returning Lord; our judge; our motivation for remaining faithful. Paul has been captured and liberated by Jesus, and he wants us to know that.

As we study Paul's letters to Timothy and Titus, it is appropriate to focus upon that same Jesus. Christ is the heart of six great themes in the Pastorals.

## I.  CHRIST IS THE HEART OF HIS CHURCH.

**A.** The Pastorals teach us to be as concerned about the church scattered for service as the church gathered for worship (2 Timothy 2:2).

**B.** The Pastorals are all concerned about leaders and followers functioning in ministry rather than appointment to an office (1 Timothy 3; Titus 1).

## II.  CHRIST IS THE HEART OF OUR DEVOTION.

**A.** When Paul wrote, "I urge, then, first of all, that requests, prayers, intercession and thanksgiving be made for everyone" (1 Timothy 2:1), he was calling us to follow the dynamic prayer example of Jesus.

**B.** The Pastorals emphasize both our private and public worship.

## III. CHRIST IS THE HEART OF GODLY CHRISTIAN LIVING.

**A.** The Word of God became flesh and dwelt among us; he showed us what God is like and how to live for him (John 1:14).

**B.** The Pastorals teach us that the character of God is the moral standard of the universe, and he wants us to be like him—godly.

**C.** The Pastorals also give us a vivid description of what it means to be ungodly (2 Timothy 3:1-5).

**D.** The bottom line: "godliness with contentment is great gain" (1 Timothy 6:6).

## IV. CHRIST IS THE HEART OF THE GREAT COMMISSION.

**A.** The Bible is a Great Commission Bible because it is all about Christ as the heart of the commission.

**B.** He preexisted with God the Father when God gave his Great Commission to Abraham in Genesis 12:1-3.

**C.** The Gospels and Acts make it clear how Jesus carried out the commission and passed it on to us.

**D.** The churches at Ephesus and Crete are Great Commission churches with a global outreach (1 Timothy 2:1-7).

## V. CHRIST IS THE HEART OF OUR MESSAGE.

**A.** Our task is to be a herald—to deliver the king's message faithfully without altering it.

**B.** Our message is about him: preexisting, virgin born, his life and teachings, his death and resurrection, his ascension, his living presence, his second coming, and his certain judgment of the living and the dead.

**C.** Paul's summary of the gospel is the person of Christ (2 Timothy 2:8).

**D.** We must teach healthy doctrine with faith and love (2 Timothy 1:13, 14).

## VI. CHRIST IS THE HEART OF OUR FUTURE.

**A.** Christ promised he would return (John 14:1-4).

**B.** We are to live our lives conscious of living between the first and second advents of Christ (Titus 2:11-15).

**C.** Christ died for us, he lives for us, and he will be there at journey's end for us (2 Timothy 4:6-8).

# A Church That Pleases God
## (An Overview Sermon)

### 1 Timothy 3:14-16

To use J. B. Phillips's term, the Pastorals are "Letters to Young Churches." They are a missionary's letters to mission churches, reminding them about why they are there and what to do about it. Those are not bad reminders for the church at any time in any era.

The purpose of this sermon is to provide an overview of the Pastoral Epistles and to introduce a course of sermons on them. It is impossible to cover all three letters in one sermon, but it is possible to look at key ideas that stretch all the way from Ephesus to Crete and from the first century to the twenty-first. Paul uses these four key ideas to arm the church, then and now, as it confronts an increasingly pagan society.

## I. THE FIRST WORD IS "CHURCH."

**A.** The church is difficult to describe biblically because twentieth-century institutionalism gets read back into the Pastorals. (Our emphasis is too often on the church gathered for worship and too little on the church scattered.)

**B.** Biblical descriptions of the church (1 Timothy 3:15).
1. The church is the household of God.
2. The church belongs to the living God—as opposed to false gods of any kind.
3. The church is the pillar and ground of the truth.
   a. "The foundation of the truth" can refer to either the foundation of a building or to the buttress that stabilizes it. (We are to confirm the gospel.)
   b. "The pillar of the truth" is illustrated vividly by the Temple of Artemis in Ephesus, one of the seven wonders of the ancient world. It had 100 Ionic columns, each 58 feet high, holding up a massive shining marble roof that could be seen far and wide. (We are to lift the gospel up for all to see.)

**C.** The church is to take a stand against false doctrine.
1. False teachers and false teachings threaten, then and now, to topple the global proclamation of the gospel.
2. The opposite of false teaching is sound or healthy teaching.

## II. THE SECOND WORD IS "HEART."

A. Paul refers twice to "a pure heart" in the Pastorals (1 Timothy 1:5; 2 Timothy 2:22).

B. "Heart" appears 148 times in the New Testament, 814 times in the Old Testament (400 of these refer to the mind).

C. More than the center of emotions, the biblical heart stands for the whole of one's inner being—mind, emotions, conscience, and will.

D. More than converting a person to a certain way of thinking, it calls for a surrender of our total being to God.

## III. THE THIRD WORD IS "GODLINESS."

A. The context of 1 Timothy 3:14-16 is about how we ought to behave in the church, including the beliefs and behavior of church leaders.

B. True faith can never be separated from true living.

C. Godliness includes both a commitment to a holy life and to the Great Commission of Christ—both piety and proclamation.

D. The false teachers were characterized by their godless lives. (The final test of your belief is how it affects your behavior.)

## IV. THE FOURTH WORD IS "CHRIST."

A. Christ is the heart of the Pastorals and the heart of the church.

B. There are many marvelous truths that we are to proclaim, but ultimate truth is in Christ (Ephesians 4:20; John 14:6).

C. He did what none of the philosophers in Ephesus or Athens could do: he brought a saving word from outside, and that has made all the difference.

D. Truth finds its center in him.

E. Godliness is defined by his example and teachings.

F. The righteous and loving heart of God is laid open to us in Christ.

## CONCLUSION

Our life is lived out on a bigger stage than this world; the message of the Pastorals is the only thing that can get us ready to stand before him as the righteous judge when he comes again (Titus 2:11-14; 2 Timothy 4:7, 8).

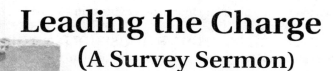

# Leading the Charge
## (A Survey Sermon)

### *1 Timothy*

One way of getting a feel for 1 Timothy is to look for the pressing issues highlighted in the letter and to see where they apply to our lives today. Paul is writing practical advice to Timothy, his companion in ministry and beloved son in the faith, but it is not a private letter. He intended it to be read to the whole church for two purposes: to throw his apostolic weight behind Timothy's ministry and to let the Christians at Ephesus know what was expected of them. It is not a private letter in another sense: it was meant for us as well as Timothy, and for our church as well as the one in Ephesus.

With that in mind, it is important, in turn, to see the letter at two overlapping levels: the specific responsibilities of church leadership, and the more general responsibilities of every member of the church. A word of warning: it is common for scholars to put the emphasis of the letter on the gathered church at worship and not to see Paul's wider emphasis on the scattered church living out their Christian walk in every area of life. True, his words include the public assembly of the church, but they also address how we are to act as members of the church living in the world.

We can get a better grasp of the letter's impact by looking at the problems the church at Ephesus faced and the five-fold charge that Paul gave to Timothy.

## I. DOCTRINE IN GOD'S HOUSEHOLD (1:1-20)
    **A.** The problem: False doctrine compromises the truth of the church's message.
        1. Christians must avoid following those devoted to false doctrines (1:1-11).
        2. Nevertheless, the life of Paul illustrates that even the worst false teacher can turn from false teaching and be used by God (1:12-17).

    **B.** The solution: Fight the good fight of faith, taking truth seriously (1:18-20).

## II. BEHAVIOR IN GOD'S HOUSEHOLD (2:1–3:16)
    **A.** The problem: Inappropriate behavior undermines the witness of the church.
        1. The church must be united in prayer for others (2:1-7).
        2. Men must channel their energy toward prayer rather than aggression and anger (2:8).
        3. Women must concentrate upon propriety, living in faith, love, and holiness (2:9-15).
        4. Both elders and deacons must be known for behavior that demonstrates godliness (3:1-13).

**B.** The solution: Teach the church proper behavior so it will be recognized for what it is—the pillar and foundation of the truth (3:14-16).

## III. FALSE TEACHERS IN GOD'S HOUSEHOLD (4:1-16)

**A.** The problem: False teachers bring confusion into the church.

  1. The false teachers are hypocritical liars, without conscience. They are deceptive and demonic in their teachings, forbidding marriage and the eating of certain foods. They are wrong in what they say and wrong in what they do (4:1-5).
  2. True teachers are to teach the truths of the faith and train themselves to be godly (4:6-10).

**B.** The solution: Watch your life and doctrine closely and don't neglect the exercise of your gift. Show that your doctrine is pure by showing that your life is pure (4:11-16).

## VI. RELATIONSHIPS IN GOD'S HOUSEHOLD (5:1-25)

**A.** The problem: Broken relationships threaten the unity of the church.

  1. Treat all people fairly, respecting their needs (5:1, 2).
  2. Make sure to care properly for widows (5:3-16).
  3. Treat elders with honor and respect (5:17-20).

**B.** The solution: Treat people according to the counsel of the Word of God without partiality. Do nothing out of favoritism (5:21-25).

## V. ATTITUDES IN GOD'S HOUSEHOLD (6:1-21)

**A.** The problem: Selfish attitudes weaken the focus of the church.

  1. The believer's job is to be the best servant he can be (6:1, 2).
  2. One's possessions should never replace God as a source of security. One should be content with what he has and thank God for it. Furthermore, he should be rich toward God and use what he has wisely for the glory of God (6:3-19).

**B.** The solution: Guard what has been entrusted to your care; avoid godless chatter and confusing ideas (6:20, 21).

## CONCLUSION

Paul's advice to Timothy can be summarized simply. In leading the charge in a healthy congregation, *serve responsibly*. Serve responsibly because we carry out our ministry as Christians in the sight of our life-giving God and before Christ Jesus. Serve responsibly because of the example of Jesus who stood firm in his testimony before Pontius Pilate. Serve responsibly because Christ is coming again right on time. God guarantees it.

# The Healthy Church
## (A Book Sermon)

### 1 Timothy 1:12-17

At first glance our text looks like an afterthought. A closer look, however, reveals that it is the central theme of the letter and, beyond that, the core of the Christian faith.

Paul follows the formula of his day for drafting an important letter. A thanksgiving section often appeared near the beginning containing the threads of the themes woven throughout the letter. Here it follows the greeting and is sandwiched between a double warning dealing decisively with false teachers and false teachings.

The testimony of thanksgiving does something else: it keeps the main thing the main thing. It makes teaching the truth more important than exposing and fighting false teachings. Look at the reasons this text gives us for giving thanks to Christ.

## I. THANKS BE TO CHRIST FOR SHOWING US WE ARE SINNERS (1:13).

**A.** We are not always as clear about our sinful status as we ought to be.

1. It was clear to Paul: he was once a blasphemer, a persecutor, a violent man—the chief of sinners.
2. But he did it in ignorance and unbelief: we are playing with double-forked lightning when we knowingly, willfully, and arrogantly take our stand against the things of Christ.

**B.** Paul's story is his own, but it is also our story.

## II. THANKS BE TO CHRIST FOR BEING WILLING TO SAVE SINNERS LIKE US (1:14, 15).

**A.** It is so important that Paul labels it a "trustworthy saying that deserves full acceptance." No way does he want us to miss it.

**B.** The trustworthy saying is this: "Christ Jesus came into the world to save sinners." It echoes the words of Jesus: "For the Son of Man came to seek and to save what was lost" (Luke 19:10).

**C.** There are two things we must never forget—the memory of our sin and the memory of when he saved us.

1. The memory of our sin by itself leaves us feeling guilty and defeated.

2. The memory of our salvation renews the freshness of God's grace, mercy, faith, and love poured out in Christ.

## III. THANKS BE TO CHRIST FOR LETTING REDEEMED SINNERS LIKE US SERVE HIM (1:12).

**A.** Christ gives us the strength to serve him; we are not on our own.

**B.** Christ trusts us to serve him faithfully; we dare not betray that trust.

**C.** Christ has appointed us to his service; we are his special servants by divine appointment.

## IV. THANKS BE TO CHRIST FOR USING THE TRANSFORMATION IN OUR LIVES TO LEAD OTHERS TO HIM (1:16).

**A.** The best argument for Christianity is still a transformed life.

**B.** Paul's transformation like ours did not come in a day; it is the result of God's endless patience.

**C.** God still uses the account of Paul as Exhibit A—a preliminary model of what he wants to do with everyone right on the edge of trusting him forever. It's like Paul is saying, "If he can do what he did for me, Timothy, he can do it for anyone."

## V. THANKS BE TO CHRIST FOR HIS GRACE THAT LETS US EXPRESS OUR GRATITUDE TO GOD (1:17).

**A.** With all its warnings, Paul's message is doxological; it is laced with praise to God.

**B.** He teaches us to put the focus on God where it belongs.
1. Praise God who is eternal—beyond the limits of time.
2. Praise God who is immortal—beyond the limits of death and the grave.
3. Praise God who is invisible—beyond every limit we can see.
4. Praise God who is the only God—vastly beyond the limit of any competition for our allegiance.

## CONCLUSION

To have a healthy church, **keep the main thing the main thing.** Don't let anyone or anything take your hallelujah from you. Whatever midnight prison holds you captive, don't forget to pray and sing praises to God. Fight the good fight. Stay in it for the long haul. It is a campaign we are in and not just a single battle. Hold on to the true faith—if we lose that, we will fall for whatever is popular. Hold a good conscience—without it you lose your integrity, your influence, and your salvation.

# The Healthy Church
## (Hold Healthy Convictions)

### *1 Timothy 1*

A healthy church can be described as a teaching-learning fellowship, and healthy leaders and healthy followers are both essential to the process. Followership is so important for two reasons: 1) You cannot be a leader if no one is following, and 2) God wants to turn gifted followers into capable leaders. His "Exhibit A" is the way he raised up Paul and made him into a godly leader, and his "Exhibit B" is the way he raised up Timothy through the mentoring of Paul.

The behavior of leaders and followers in preserving sound doctrine is a major theme in Paul's first letter to Timothy. Preserving healthy doctrine and avoiding diseased doctrine in the church must be extremely important to God because his apostle mentions it so often in this letter. He tells us how to guard the good news about Jesus Christ and to pass it on to others. His strategy is to insure that we preserve healthy doctrine by giving us a series of warnings against unhealthy doctrines.

## I. DON'T LET THE CHURCH DRIFT INTO FALSE TEACHING (1:3).

**A.** This was Paul's reason for leaving Timothy in Ephesus, and it is why God has leaders in the local congregation.

**B.** We must understand what the Bible means by "avoiding false teaching."
1. It does not mean that we always understand everything alike.
2. It does mean that we are not divisive over our opinions.
3. It does not mean that we always have to prove our point.
4. It does mean that we do not preach and teach another gospel. (The word "hetero" means "different from.")

**C.** We must not teach heresy (a different doctrine) nor allow heresy to be taught to the church.

## II. DON'T GET SIDETRACKED BY SPECULATIVE IDEAS (1:3, 4).

**A.** There are all kinds of questions the Bible does not address that are fun to speculate about, but they take us nowhere.

**B.** There are all kinds of weird interpretations that imaginative people can read into almost any biblical passage to promote their ideas instead of keeping to the point of the gospel.

**C.** The fanciful use of Scripture not only leads one away from the centrality of the gospel, it breeds controversy that results in God's work not getting done.

## III. DON'T SWERVE FROM THE GOAL OF YOUR TEACHING (1:5).

**A.** Our goal is to produce love out of a clean heart.

**B.** Our goal is to produce love out of a good conscience.

**C.** Our goal is to produce love out of a sincere faith.

## IV. DON'T ENGAGE IN FRUITLESS DISCUSSIONS (1:6, 7).

**A.** Warning: Some teachers who act confident do not know the gospel.

**B.** Some teachings pervert the purpose of the Law which is to expose diseased doctrine and to condemn opposition to healthy doctrine. Some teachings seek to justify sin, but God gave the Law to condemn sin. God gave us a catalogue of sins so that we would not miss the point, and so that we could spot the diseased teaching of false teachers.

## V. DON'T IGNORE THE EXAMPLE OF TEACHERS YOU CAN TRUST (ILLUSTRATED IN THE LIFE OF PAUL—1:12-17).

**A.** The testimony of service for Christ results from his grace.
   1. Christ graciously gave Paul strength for his work.
   2. He graciously trusted Paul for his work.
   3. He graciously appointed Paul to his work.

**B.** The testimony of salvation through Christ that you cannot argue with—a completely transformed life (Paul's testimony).
   1. He considered himself the chief of sinners.
   2. He had been deeply religious but was also a blasphemer, a persecutor, and a violent man.
   3. He was treated mercifully because he did not know what he was doing or whom he was doing it against.
   4. He became Exhibit A before the eyes of a watching world to demonstrate to those on the edge of becoming a Christian what God in his patience is able to do for them.

**C.** The testimony of joyful praise that is a beautiful doxology to the one who gives eternal life.

## CONCLUSION

We have heard the warning against false teachers and their diseased doctrine. We have gazed at the ministry and conversion of one of the greatest Christian leaders of all time. But there is one more thing we must hear. We must fight the good fight by holding the faith in a good conscience.

# The Healthy Church
## (Pray Healthy Prayers)

### 1 Timothy 2

How we relate to God in our prayer lives goes a long way in determining how healthy we are as a congregation. God wants us to do many things as Christians besides pray, but he does not want us to do anything else until we pray.

Healthy prayers—the prayers that please God most—extend around the globe. They ask God to bless many people whom we will never know personally because they belong to the people groups of the world that Jesus commissioned his church to evangelize (Matthew 28:16-20). They are healthy prayers because they take us outside ourselves, and they focus on the heartbeat of God—to win the peoples of the world back to him and to enfold them into healthy congregations of believers.

There is an interesting cycle at work here. Healthy prayers are prayed by healthy congregations, and by their nature members of healthy congregations pray for their own needs and the needs of each other. They must in order to be a healthy congregation. But they do not stop there. They pray for the reached and unreached around the world. Why are we to pray for the people groups of the world? The answers to that question are embedded in our text.

## I. PRAY FOR THEM BECAUSE WE AS CHRISTIANS ARE TO BE CONCERNED FOR ALL PEOPLES (2:1, 2).

**A.** We are instructed to pray for everyone.

**B.** We are instructed to pray for rulers and all in authority.
1. Even if we do not agree with them on major issues or respect their lifestyle.
2. Nero, the mad emperor, ruled Rome when Paul was writing.

**C.** Why then this request?
1. To save the nation from chaos and anarchy.
2. To allow us to live out our lives as godly Christians.

## II. PRAY FOR THEM BECAUSE GOD IS CONCERNED FOR ALL PEOPLES (2:3, 4).

**A.** God wants all people to be saved; he is a missionary God.

**B.** God wants all people to know the truth about him and how to live in a right relationship with him through Christ.

## III. PRAY FOR THEM BECAUSE CHRIST IS CONCERNED FOR ALL PEOPLES (2:5, 6).

**A.** There is one God over all peoples—the man Christ Jesus came to reveal him.

**B.** There is one mediator between God and all peoples—the man Christ Jesus.

**C.** There is one Savior that God has appointed for all peoples—the man Christ Jesus.

## IV. PRAY FOR THEM BECAUSE THE GOSPEL IS CONCERNED FOR ALL PEOPLES (2:7).

**A.** God calls us by divine appointment to announce the good news of Christ.

**B.** God calls us to teach the true faith that accompanies the good news.

**C.** God calls us to share that message with all peoples (Gentiles).

## V. PRAY FOR THEM BECAUSE WE AS CHRISTIAN MEN AND WOMEN ARE TO BE CONCERNED FOR ALL PEOPLES (2:8-15).

**A.** Our behavior as Christian men is to be consistent with our prayers (2:8).
   1. We are to pray with "holy hands." Lifting our hands is not the only posture for prayer; rather our prayers are to come from clean hearts.
   2. We are to pray without anger in our hearts or disputes on our lips.

**B.** Our behavior as Christian women is to be consistent with our prayers (2:9-15).
   1. Clothing, hairstyles, and jewelry are not to be extravagant, vain, or suggestive.
   2. The best clothing and makeup are to be good deeds that flow out of reverence for God.
   3. Conduct is to be marked by a humility that does not try to take over or tell the men what to do.
   4. Attitude is to be quiet and obedient along with everyone else.
   5. Salvation is secure but only if one continues in faith, love, and holiness.

**C.** Reverence for God and healthy relationships between men and women are essential for a healthy congregation and for its healthy global prayer life.

## CONCLUSION

God is a prayer answering God, and he will bless the prayers of a healthy church in a special way. He will bless us as we pray, he will bless those for whom we pray, and he will continue to bless the mission of a healthy congregation.

# The Healthy Church
## (Choose Healthy Leaders)

### *1 Timothy 3*

There are many sub-quality leaders who act like wonderful teachers but know nothing about the gospel then or now. What our text says about the qualities of good leaders is especially important when we view it against the backdrop of these false teachers.

Choosing quality leaders is everyone's responsibility in the congregation, and the standard of quality is to be the Word of God. Look at the three groups of healthy leaders named here.

I. **HEALTHY ELDERS ARE THOSE WHO ARE KNOWN FOR THEIR ABILITY TO NURTURE (3:1-7).**
   **A.** Misunderstandings about the eldership:
   1. It is not an office (though not in the Greek text, the word "office" appears in many English translations) but rather a work to be accomplished.
   2. It is not for the immature but rather for the tested and proven.
   3. It is not for those seeking prestige and honor but rather for those desiring to serve.

   **B.** The characteristics of a quality elder:
   1. His personal life must be "above reproach"—the hallmark against which the other characteristics are measured. He is to be temperate, self-controlled, respectable, not given to drunkenness, not violent, not quarrelsome, not a lover of money.
   2. He must manage the affairs of his own household well: be committed to his wife, be attentive to his children and be respected by them, and be hospitable.
   3. He must have a good reputation with outsiders in order to influence them toward Christ and in order not to fall into the devil's trap in disgrace.
   4. He must be able to teach. (Teaching is always important, but because of the reputation that false teachers were giving the church, the accent is on the quality of an elder's life.)

II. **HEALTHY DEACONS AND DEACONESSES ARE THOSE WHO SERVE IN SPECIAL WAYS (3:8-13).**
   **A.** Deacons are the men who serve the church in special ways. (Their tasks are

to serve the congregation, but the emphasis here is on character.)
1. Their qualities are basically the same as those for elders except for two that are added—they are not to be double-tongued, and they are to hold the deep truths of the faith with a clear conscience.
2. Their behavior is to be an effective contrast to that of the false teachers and their falsehoods.

B. Deaconesses are the women who serve the church in special ways.
1. "In the same way" (3:11) seems to indicate that the women mentioned here are the female counterpart of deacons.
2. Some versions translate the Scripture "wives" of deacons. In either circumstance, they would serve alongside the deacons.
3. In addition to the other standards, they are not to be malicious talkers or gossips.

C. Their reward is twofold:
1. They gain a good reputation through their service.
2. They draw closer to God through their service.

## III. HEALTHY MEMBERS ARE ALL THOSE WHO BELONG TO THE COMPANY OF THE COMMITTED (3:14-16).
A. The objective of healthy leadership is to create healthy followership so that the whole church is always in process of becoming what God intended.

B. How we behave as Christians makes or breaks the witness of the church in the community.

C. Why proper behavior in the church is so important:
1. It is God's household.
2. It belongs to the one and only living God.
3. It is the pillar and foundation of the truth.
4. Christ, the head of the church, is worthy to be praised and proclaimed to all the ends of the earth.

## CONCLUSION
Healthy leaders bring together in themselves the essential core of Christian truth (faith) and the essential code of Christian conduct (godliness). This core and code are the only protection for the church, and, with God's blessing, they are enough.

Beyond laying out the high standards that elders and deacons are to meet, the code of conduct in chapter three becomes a guide to spiritual maturity for all Christians. Like a map, it points out areas that need our attention, but it also points out areas of encouragement by giving us guidelines for measuring our growth. A look at this map will keep us on track and ensure that we are in the process of developing healthy future leaders.

# The Healthy Church
## (Lead Healthy Lives)

### *1 Timothy 4*

Just as infections invade our bodies and sometimes do immeasurable harm, spiritual infections invade the body of Christ and threaten our spiritual health. 1 Timothy 4 is about religious infections that run all the way from nullifying our effectiveness as Christian servants and leaders to bringing spiritual death. Paul diagnoses three of them and tells us what to do in order to lead healthy Christian lives.

## I. INFECTIONS THAT KILL US—RELIGIOUS LIES THAT TEAR US FROM THE TRUTH (4:1-5)

**A.** God warns us that we will be threatened by religious lies and religious liars until Christ returns (Matthew 24:11; 2 Thessalonians 2:4; 2 Timothy 4:1, 2).

1. Satan is the one behind false teaching (deceiving spirits and demons), but it comes through charismatic leaders with cauterized consciences who teach attractive but diseased doctrines that end in spiritual death.

2. Satan always lies to us about sex—he either denies our sexuality and forbids us to marry or he urges us to debauch ourselves by indulging in what he calls "free love," but which really leads to the worst kind of bondage and pain.

3. Satan always lies to us about something as basic as the right kind of food. He either wants to turn us into gluttons whose god is our stomach or into health food freaks who measure our Christianity by what we do not eat.

4. Satan's lies are all around us today: the cults, the new age movement, resurgent Islam, and pagan religions—all have an element of the truth but pervert it into an attractive, deadly lie.

**B.** God takes us all the way back to creation to show us the truth (Genesis 1:26-31).

1. God created men and women in his image to marry and to propagate the earth, and he created plants and animals for food. Because he made them, they are good.

2. Not everything about the world is good since sin entered through the fall to spoil much of God's creation.

3. Receive all that God has given you in creation with prayer and thanksgiving.

## II. INFECTIONS THAT MAKE US ANEMIC—FANTASIES THAT ARE DRESSED UP AS RELIGION (4:6-10)

**A.** Folk religion or civil religion occurs when culture and tradition are mixed with Christianity.

1. Legends and traditions become more important than Scripture.
2. Ancestral pedigree and race become more important than Christian service.

**B.** Self-worship is another fantasy. It is evident in our current preoccupation with keeping our youth at all cost by diet, exercise, and cosmetics.

**C.** We respond by choosing truth over fantasy.

1. We must separate cultural allegiances and mythologies from the truth of godliness.
2. Because the body is the temple of the Holy Spirit, one is obligated as a good steward to exercise and eat wisely. Yet physical workouts have limited value, because sooner or later, everyone will die.
3. Spiritual discipline and heavenly citizenship are better because they bless us both in this life and in the life to come (4:6-9).

## III. INFECTIONS THAT MAKE US LETHARGIC—RELIGIOUS PUT-DOWNS THAT KEEP US FROM DOING OUR BEST SERVICE FOR CHRIST (4:11-15)

**A.** Others may put us down with unfair criticisms: for example, we are too young or too old to be Christian leaders.

**B.** We may put ourselves down by concentrating on what we cannot do or by not concentrating on what we *can* do.

**C.** We can respond by fighting this spiritual lethargy.

1. Silence criticism with godly conduct: your speech, life, love, faith, and purity.
2. Be faithful to your ministry: reading, preaching, and teaching the Word.
3. Keep on doing your duty and growing.
4. Watch your life and doctrine closely.

## CONCLUSION

Leading a healthy Christian life of service results in salvation—both ours and those who hear and obey our teaching. So take infection seriously. Get your nourishment, do the exercise that God prescribes, and rest in the Lord. It just might save your life—eternally.

# The Healthy Church
## (Practice Healthy Relationships)
### *1 Timothy 5*

Healthy relationships have always been important in the church, but they are especially important today. New people in our worship services are hungry for relationships. They come with a hunger for God and for meaningful contact with others. If they find them, they will stick around to listen to our message; if they don't, they leave. Their motto could be: "I will care about what you say after you show me you care."

I Timothy 5 tells us how to relate to four groups of people in the church.

## I. TREAT THE DIFFERENT GENERATIONS IN THE CHURCH WITHOUT PARTIALITY (5:1, 2).

**A.** It is comforting to know that problems with relating across the generation gap in the church have been around for twenty centuries. (We may give them new names like the gray wave, boomers, busters, generation X or Y, but the task of relating to young and old alike has always been there.)

**B.** How do you treat the different generations without partiality?
1. It does not mean to treat everyone exactly alike, because their needs and interests are different, but to treat them without favoritism.
2. We respect social boundaries with sensitivity and care; if we have to confront someone, we do it graciously without defensiveness, anger, or bitterness.
3. Treat older men and women as you would a father and mother—with respect, affection, and gentleness. (If they are unkind, it does not mean we have to be unkind.)
4. Treat younger men as brothers and younger women as sisters—as equals with tolerance and understanding. (Treat younger women as sisters with absolute sexual purity.)

## II. TREAT WIDOWS WITH COMPASSION (HOW THE CHURCH OUGHT TO CARE FOR ALL ITS NEEDY MEMBERS—5:3-16).

**A.** The church inherited a fine tradition of charity to those in need from its Jewish roots; it must never do less than its Jewish and pagan neighbors.

**B.** Widows are to be supported with honor (proper recognition) and compassion—emotionally, spiritually, and financially if they are really in need.

1. If their families are able, they are to care for their own elderly family members. The text gives four reasons: to repay our parents for caring for us, to please God, to avoid denying our faith, and to relieve the church of an unnecessary burden.
2. If they are really in need and are alone, the church is to help them as their extended Christian family.

    **C.** Widows are to serve the church according to their ability if they meet the qualifications.
1. She must be advanced in age (in that day 60 was when she was culturally past the age of remarrying and was retired).
2. She must have been faithful to her husband so that her example will be a credit to the church.
3. She must be well known for her good deeds: bringing up children, showing hospitality, willing to do humble tasks, and helping those in trouble.

## III. TREAT ELDERS WITH HONOR (5:17-20).

    **A.** Treat all elders with honor.

    **B.** Treat elders who preach and teach the Word with double honor: appropriate respect and appropriate wages.

    **C.** Require an accusation against an elder to be verified by more than one witness.

    **D.** Do not allow leaders like Hymanaeus and Alexander to continue in their sin so that the eldership may continue to be a function of honor.

## IV. TREAT YOURSELF WITH RESPECT (5:21-25).

    **A.** While you are taking care of everyone else, do not forget to take care of yourself; you cannot give out for long more than you take in.

    **B.** Minister fairly without favoritism.

    **C.** Take your time in choosing leaders.

    **D.** Take care of your physical needs.

    **E.** Leave the ultimate judgment to God: some things are obvious, others are hidden.

## CONCLUSION

How we treat each other is a clue to how we really treat Christ. At its core, Christianity is relational. It begins and ends with a personal relationship with Christ. That is where healthy Christian relationships always start.

# The Healthy Church
## (Exhibit a Healthy Attitude)
### *1 Timothy 6*

A healthy Christian attitude is a Christ-like attitude. The clearest statement of what it means to have the attitude of Christ is in Philippians 2 where Paul takes us once again to the cross. "Your attitude should be the same as that of Christ Jesus" who became a servant, humbling himself, "and became obedient to death—even death on a cross."

God wants us to have a humble Christ-like attitude toward all of the situations and circumstances of life, so that people outside the church may be attracted to Christ because they see him in us. In 1 Timothy 6 he opens up several areas where we need a Christ-like attitude.

## I. EXHIBIT A CHRIST-LIKE ATTITUDE TOWARD WORK (6:1, 2).

**A.** Our attitude toward our work determines whether God's name and the teaching of the apostles will be slandered.

**B.** Approximately one third of the population (fifteen to twenty million) of the Roman Empire were slaves.
1. They were regarded as potential enemies.
2. The church encouraged Christian slaves to give loving service to their masters: if masters were not Christians, slaves were not to look down on them; if they were Christians, slaves were not to slough off but to serve them better because both of them were believers.
3. Thus slaves helped to win the Roman Empire for Christ.

**C.** This text instructs us to show respect to our supervisors and to give them honest service so that the gospel will not be blamed.

**D.** Christ's attitude: "Love your enemies and pray for those who persecute you, that you may be sons of your Father in heaven" (Matthew 5:44, 45).

## II. EXHIBIT A CHRIST-LIKE ATTITUDE TOWARD THE TRUTH OF THE GOSPEL (6:3-5).

**A.** The sophists, the "spin doctors" of the first century, gave glowing speeches that made the worse seem better, competed for applause, and judged everything by how many came to hear their performance. False teachers, then

27

and now, spin speculative theories and arguments, cause constant friction, and use religion to make a fast buck.

**B.** Christ's attitude: "Watch out for false prophets. They come to you in sheep's clothing, but inwardly they are ferocious wolves" (Matthew 7:15).

## III. EXHIBIT A CHRIST-LIKE ATTITUDE TOWARD YOUR POSSESSIONS (6:6-10, 17-19).

**A.** The poor are to be content with what they have. They should live a godly lifestyle, a self-sufficiency independent of circumstances (6:6-8). Furthermore they must avoid the folly of covetousness. Dissatisfaction stemming from a love of material goods is a root of all kinds of evil and a terrible source of grief (6:9, 10).

**B.** The rich must see wealth as a servant, not a master (6:17-19). They must resist letting their wealth spawn arrogance. Rather, they should place their hope in God and not in riches, being rich in good deeds and extravagant generosity.

**C.** Christ's attitude: "Store up for yourselves treasures in heaven. . . . For where your treasure is, there your heart will be also. . . . You cannot serve both God and Money" (Matthew 6:20, 21, 24).

## IV. EXHIBIT A CHRIST-LIKE ATTITUDE IN YOUR MINISTRY (6:11-16, 20, 21).

**A.** Flee everything incompatible with his will.

**B.** Follow righteousness, godliness, faith, love, endurance, and gentleness.

**C.** Fight the good fight of faith to which you committed yourself when you made the good confession.

**D.** Fasten on to eternal life and never let go.

**E.** Have Christ's attitude: "You are the light of the world. . . . let your light shine before men, that they may see your good deeds and praise your Father in heaven" (Matthew 5:14, 16).

## CONCLUSION

The letter draws to a close with a name, an admonition, a warning, and a word of grace. The name Christian means one who follows Christ. The admonition is to guard the Word of God—the sacred trust given to us. The warning is to turn away from godless talk that wrecks our faith. The closing benediction reminds us that it is grace that has brought us this far and grace that will take us home.

# The Last Letter From My Father

## (A Narrative Book Sermon)
### *2 Timothy*

*Let me tell you a modern day parable:*

My name is Timothy. I grew up in a wealthy Greek family in Cleveland, Ohio. My father, Paul, who is in failing health, owns the company that his father started, and it has grown from a small family business into a private multi-billion-dollar concern. My father currently runs it, and I will inherit it from my father as he inherited it from his father. We manufacture the finest life-support system in the world. There is nothing else like it; without it people would die. Because of its life-sustaining capability, my father always considered the business not so much his to own but rather an invaluable trust to be carefully guarded and passed on safely to the next generation.

Over the last 15 years I have had hands-on experience in almost every job at our plant in Cleveland and in every branch in the United States and overseas. I recently received an E-mail from my father at our branch office in Asia where I am currently working, telling me that his health is getting steadily worse and this may be the last letter he will be able to write. His message is a double burden: in addition to my grief at his approaching death, I will have the awesome responsibility for the enterprise placed on my shoulders.

Everyone trusts my father. He has a special charisma and is a born leader, a great visionary who has taken the company beyond where anyone dreamed, and soon he will be gone. Can I do it? Can I become half the leader he is? What will happen when they compare me to my father? I inherited my mother's quiet disposition and shyness. They have been used to a hard-driving, outgoing leader with a magnetic personality, even if he does have weak eyes, is short, and no prize to look at. Will they follow me as they have him? How will I maintain morale among the workers? Can I solve problems that arise in the plants satisfactorily? How do I guarantee a quality product? Will the opposition get much worse? What will happen to the economy? How do we advertise our product honestly and attractively when the necessary cost of quality is so high and the cutthroat competition is selling a piece of junk at a fraction of the cost? What do I do about my health problems which are already showing up at 38, and what do I do about the constant knot in my stomach?

I have proven over the last 15 years that I can hang in there through tough times and do a commendable job, but can I handle this awesome responsibility?

I shall always prize my father's letter, not only because it is his last letter to me, but also because of the business plan he included and strongly urged me to adopt.

1. Keep our product pure and of the highest quality. You cannot improve on it and nothing will ever compare with it, but you will have to present it accurately and market it with sensitivity to the people for whom it is a matter of life and death.

2. Never give in to the pressures of our competitors. Combat their efforts by teaching everyone about our standard of integrity from the beginning. Point out our track record and compare it to the record of our opposition who promise the moon and fleece the unsuspecting with a product that does not last.

3. Keep morale high among your workers by demonstrating faith in them. Show love and respect for them as individuals and for what they do for the company, and always live so that your conscience is clear before God and men. Perhaps it should not be so, but some will stay with the company only if you demonstrate integrity and create high morale among them.

4. It may sound out of place in a business plan, but bring God into this. You were brought up to make Christ your partner in everything you do. I can tell you that it is his grace that will sustain you in the tough times ahead. He has been my senior partner for years.

5. Guard your inheritance well and make your plans now to begin to prepare your son or daughter to inherit what I am passing on to you. That is what I want and it is what God desires of you.

6. My personal mission statement is 2 Timothy 1:14, "Guard the good deposit that was entrusted to you—guard it with the help of the Holy Spirit who lives in us."

7. And because he is my senior partner, this statement is also precious as I think about leaving you: "I am not ashamed, because I know whom I have believed, and am convinced that he is able to guard what I have entrusted to him for that day" (2 Timothy 1:12).

With God's help you can do what he has called you to do. And we will see each other again—in my father's mansion.

# Hanging Tough
## (Surviving a Rough World)

### *2 Timothy 1*

Paul felt the ache that every decent parent or Christian feels—you want desperately to help those you love who are struggling to hang in there in their effort to turn obstacles into personal and public victories. It is all the more important when you are about to leave this life and must entrust your legacy to younger, less confident hands.

It is a testimony of his power when all God used was a piece of parchment, a pen and bottle of ink, an apostle in a Roman prison cell about to die—and Jesus.

This chapter gives us three secrets of hanging in there in a rough world.

## I. REMEMBER HOW GOD HAS BLESSED YOU IN THE PAST (1:1-7).

**A.** Remember those who are praying constantly for you.

**B.** Remember those who love you in the Lord very much.

**C.** Remember those who passed the faith on to you.

**D.** Remember to "fan into flame" the spirit of power, love, and self-discipline that God has given you.

## II. BE WILLING, WITH GOD'S HELP, TO SUFFER FOR THE TRUTH (1:8, 9).

**A.** Be willing to take your share of suffering.
1. God will sustain you by his power. That power is supplied for the purpose of enabling you to spread the gospel, not to make your life comfortable.
2. God has saved you by his grace, not by your efforts. That favor remains regardless of your circumstances. He still loves you.
3. God has called you to a holy life. God will take care of the rest.

**B.** Do not be ashamed to speak up for the Lord.

**C.** Do not be ashamed of your fellow servants in the cause of Christ.

## III. TRUST IN CHRIST WHO IS FAITHFUL (1:10-14).

**A.** He has destroyed death for us.

**B.** He has brought life and immortality.

**C.** We must be willing to do our duty for him.
1. Paul was appointed as a herald, one who announces the good news. He furthermore was appointed as an apostle, one set aside for a particular task. Finally, he was given the role of teacher, fully equipping those in his care. We are obligated by the same gospel.
2. Paul suffered for the gospel, even as he wrote to Timothy from "death row." We may be called to do likewise.
3. Paul entrusted all that he had, his life, his reputation, his ministry, into the sure hand of God. We can do no less.

## CONCLUSION

Contrast those who abandoned Paul in prison with those who stood by him, and mark how God continues to sustain his children in difficult times (1:15-18).

Almost everyone in the province of Asia had deserted him, including Phygelus and Hermogenes, and that surely made his imprisonment almost intolerable. How lonely and abandoned he must have felt. It is tragic to have fair-weather friends, but it is doubly tragic when those friends are Christian brothers and sisters.

Onesiphorus' name, however, will be remembered and honored forever because of what he did for Paul. "He often refreshed me and was not ashamed of my chains," Paul wrote with a joyous flourish. "On the contrary, when he was in Rome, he searched hard for me until he found me." And then he remembers Onesiphorus with a double blessing: "May the Lord show mercy to his household for what he did for me, and may the Lord grant him mercy from the Lord on that day as he has shown me mercy."

But there was one other who visited Paul in his prison cell and showed him mercy; in fact, he stayed with Paul and never left him alone. His name is Jesus, and he always honors his faithful servants with his presence. "Jesus Christ came into my cell last night," cried a Scottish Covenanter imprisoned for his faith, "and every stone flashed like a ruby." He was there for Paul and he is there for you in your darkest hour. And if you have never invited him into your prison cell, why don't you do it today?

# Hanging Tough
## (Being a Strong Disciple)
### *2 Timothy 2*

It is not always easy to be a Christian. Timothy discovered that and so will we. In fact, the Christian life is so tough at times that we will not make it through without the strength that comes from the grace of Christ operating in our lives. What he calls us **to**, he will grace us **for**.

Like Timothy, our calling as Christians is to guard the gospel "deposit" faithfully and to entrust it to reliable disciples who will, in turn, pass it on. And we have to pay the price to leave this legacy to others.

2 Timothy 2 gives us six pictures that illustrate how to be a disciple that hangs tough.

## I. BE A DEDICATED SOLDIER FOR CHRIST (2:3, 4).

**A.** A good soldier is willing to endure hardship. (Christ never calls us to be "summer soldiers.")

**B.** A good soldier frees himself from any entanglements that prevent him from doing his duty.

**C.** A good soldier is always at the disposal of his commanding officer.

## II. BE A RULE-ABIDING ATHLETE FOR CHRIST (2:5).

**A.** Keep the rules of the race.
1. An athlete in the Olympics typically completes ten months of training.
2. "According to the rules" designates the athlete who trains professionally. The Christian life is not for weekend athletes. It requires consistent moral conduct and service.

**B.** Enjoy the rewards of the race.
1. A race run well are lives lived productively for God.
2. The victor's crown is promised the crown of life (James 1:12).

## III. BE A HARDWORKING FARMER FOR CHRIST (2:6).

**A.** The rigors of the task are great.
1. The farmer must work hard to be successful. Likewise, there is no easy way to be a growing Christian.

2. Paul never expected more of others than he was willing to do himself.

**B.** The rewards of the harvest are worth the work.
1. The first share of the harvest goes to the one who sowed.
2. If we sow righteousness, we reap a holy life.
3. If we sow the Word of God, we reap converts.

## IV. BE AN UNASHAMED WORKMAN FOR CHRIST (2:14-19).

**A.** A good workman correctly handles the Word of truth. This literally refers to a road that cuts a straight path through the countryside.

**B.** Therefore, the person who is accurate and plain in handling the Scriptures stays on the path and makes it easy for others to follow.

**C.** A bad workman ought to be ashamed.
1. A false teacher teaches false doctrine and indulges in godless chatter.
2. Hymenaeus and Philetus were such corrupt workmen. They taught that the resurrection had already taken place.
3. False doctrine spreads like gangrene and destroys the faith of some.

## V. BE A CLEAN VESSEL FOR CHRIST (2:20-22).

**A.** Noble vessels serve the gospel to others. Such a holy calling is to be desired.
1. To be such a vessel we must flee evil desires.
2. A noble servant pursues righteousness, faith, love, and peace.

**B.** Vessels without honor dishonor the gospel.
1. They indulge in foolish arguments.
2. They produce quarrels.

## VI. BE A FAITHFUL SERVANT OF THE LORD (2:23-26).

**A.** Do not quarrel.

**B.** Be kind to everyone.

**C.** Be able to teach.

**D.** Do not be resentful.

## CONCLUSION

One more picture helps us hang tough. Picture Jesus raised from the dead, descended from David, the resurrected King of kings (2:8). Never lose sight of him. He provides the vision for sticking it out as a Christian in a tough world.

# Hanging Tough

## (Triumph in Troubled Times)

### *2 Timothy 3*

In spite of how much we want to avoid them, I can promise you that tough times will come. It does not make it any easier that our culture pampers us with a self-centered view of ourselves and our lifestyle. The church is much like a shopping mall for many: pick out the store you like because it offers you the best deal and promises you the most goodies. We are big on wearing the crown, but we shy away from carrying the cross.

The biggest task we face is how to get through the tough times victoriously. I am not talking only about obstacles in life to overcome with a positive attitude, brains, and hard work. I am talking about overcoming the evil one who is out to destroy us and those we love. A comfortable Christianity that avoids the hard choices of belief and behavior that Christ calls us to make will not see us through the hard times.

## I. THE PROBLEM: TROUBLED TIMES ALWAYS LIE AHEAD (3:1-9).

**A.** We live in troubled times.
  1. Paul warned, "There will be terrible times in the last days" (3:1).
  2. The "last days" are the days we live in—the period between the first coming of Christ and the second (Acts 2:14-17).

**B.** The times are troubled by trouble makers (3:2-9).
  1. Their long list of offenses read like "wanted posters" of Christian criminals.
  2. Paul wants Timothy to know the true natures of these heretics so that he will have nothing to do with them (3:5).
  3. Like Jannes and Jambres who opposed the truth with depraved minds in Moses' day, these troublemakers will not get very far. They both reject and are rejected by the true faith. Their folly will become clear to everyone (3:8, 9).
  4. Paul offers this summary of their pretense: They have "a form of godliness" but deny its power (3:5).

**C.** Because of troublemakers, some become troubled (3:6, 7).
  1. People who are weak-willed and swallow every new idea are especially susceptible.
  2. Paul singles out a group of problem women, not because he is a chauvin-

ist, but because they are the strategic target of the false teachers.

3. They are loaded down with sins and evil desires. (Unrepented and unresolved sinful baggage coupled with evil desires spell trouble.)

4. Paul offers this summary of their problem: They are "always learning but never able to acknowledge the truth" (3:7).

## II. THE SOLUTION: STICK WITH WHAT YOU HAVE LEARNED AND BELIEVED (3:10-17).

**A.** Practice what you learned from your mentor. Paul mentors us as well as Timothy through this letter. Good mentors are essential for growth.

1. A good mentor's life is consistent with the gospel.

2. A good mentor demonstrates a willingness to suffer if necessary. Suffering is necessary for two reasons. One, there are some things worth any price. A pure, unadulterated gospel is certainly one of them. Two, there will always be unscrupulous people who will exploit the faith and persecute God's people.

**B.** Practice what you have learned from the Word of God.

1. The reference is to the Old Testament because the New Testament had not yet been completed, but what he said is doubly true of the New Testament.

2. The "God-breathed" Old Testament, coupled with Paul's apostolic interpretation of it in light of the gospel, gave Timothy everything a Christian leader needs. The inspired Word leads us and others to salvation, trains in right living, and equips for Christian service.

## CONCLUSION

The fact is there will always be cycles of trying times until Jesus comes again. It is the one way that we know that we are living faithful Christian lives because "everyone who wants to live a godly life in Christ Jesus will be persecuted" (3:12). And those who persecute God's people will go from bad to worse, deceiving and being deceived.

But we can get through tough times. We can persevere and overcome by the power of the Lord who rescues us and strengthens us by his grace (3:11).

It finally comes down to this: It is his battle and he is not going to lose. Be assured of that and stick with what you have learned and believed.

# Hanging Tough
## (Delivering God's Message)

*2 Timothy 4*

*A rubber message delivered by a plastic messenger will never do.* It is fitting and instructive that Paul's last words to Timothy in the closing section of his letter put the accent on declaring a tough message for tough times. The task is so important that Paul gave it as his final charge to Timothy: "In the presence of God and of Christ Jesus, who will judge the living and the dead, and in view of his appearing and his kingdom, I give you this charge: Preach the Word" (4:1, 2).

To get the message out to the whole world is the task of the whole church. He describes it as an urgent message proclaimed by persistent messengers who declare it when it is easy and when it is not, when people listen and when they do not, when they accept it and when they do not, and when they revere the messenger and when they do not.

He stresses that the message is faithful and true, and just as important, the messenger must be faithful and true both in delivering it and living it. We need to encourage each other by reminding ourselves that the gospel of Christ is tough enough to endure through the ages. It always has and it always will. Look at the four ways our text describes the message of the gospel.

## I. IT IS A MESSAGE THAT MEETS PEOPLE WHERE THEY ARE.
**A.** The message is the Word of God (4:2).
1. The Bible is the written Word of God (3:16).
2. Jesus is the living Word of God who became flesh and dwelt among us (John 1:1, 14).
3. The gospel is the Word of God we proclaim.

**B.** The messenger is the king's "herald," commissioned to deliver the king's message in the best possible way without altering it in any way.

**C.** The Word of God meets the needs of its hearers in four ways.
1. If they need to be taught, it instructs them with the words of life.
2. If they need to be convinced, it convicts them in their hearts.
3. If they need to be reproved for their sins, it has stern, warning words to bring them back to God.
4. If their hearts are weighed down and discouraged, it has words of lasting encouragement.

## II. IT IS A MESSAGE THAT CONFRONTS THE VALUES OF THIS AGE.

**A.** The Bible says, "For the time will come"—that time is now.

**B.** It also says that people will "turn their ears away from the truth and turn aside to myths"—because they prefer the values of this world rather than the values of the kingdom of God.

**C.** They will gather around them "a great number of teachers to say what their itching ears want to hear"—because they will not put up with sound doctrine.

## III. IT IS A MESSAGE WITH ETERNAL CONSEQUENCES.

**A.** It changes how we live and that affects us for eternity.

**B.** It changes how we die and that affects our eternity.

**C.** Our eternal reward—the crown of righteousness—hangs in the balance.

**D.** Demas is a case study in the eternal consequences of this message—he deserted Paul because he loved this world.

## IV. IT IS A MESSAGE THAT DEMANDS THE BEST WE CAN GIVE IT.

**A.** Our best study—Paul asked Timothy to bring the scrolls and especially the parchments.

**B.** Our best service—Gifted colleagues were serving Christ all over the Roman Empire.

**C.** Our best encouragement—Paul was a champion encourager, but he also needed encouragement.

**D.** Our best efforts to declare it— we must guard against those who oppose our message, like Alexander, the metalworker (4:14, 15). We must proclaim the message fully so that all Gentiles might hear it (4:16, 17). And finally, we must trust God to stand at our side as we proclaim it (4:17).

## CONCLUSION

We began with the message and the messenger. We conclude with the message and the hearers. This is how tough the message is: It has the power to save us, to satisfy our deepest needs, to sustain us through all of life's struggles, and to take us home safely when life here is over. It is a priceless treasure that Christ gave to his church and no one else has it. It promises that God will rescue us from every evil attack and bring us to his heavenly kingdom (4:17, 18). It can be yours. It is his gift to you. All he asks in return is your life and your loyalty and your obedience in receiving it.

# Why Build the Church?
## (A Book Sermon)

### Titus 1:1-4

Why aren't more people meaningfully involved in the church today? George Hunter writes of four barriers to church growth in a secular society. The first is an image barrier. People view worship services as boring and irrelevant. The second is a cultural barrier. The church offers music, vocabulary, rituals, and offerings that are foreign to many today. Third is a gospel barrier. Too many churches concentrate on fine doctrinal points instead of applying the good news to life. Finally, there is a commitment barrier. People who have been told that they can have it all are unwilling to commit to a faith that requires sacrifice rather than indulgence.

Lyle Schaller points out that even within the church involvement is minimal. He claims that one-third of all church members are outside the circle of meaningful membership. He lists a number of reasons for lack of involvement by those who are church members in name only. Expectations of themselves and everyone else may be too high, so they seek perfection before they get involved. Or their view of the church is too low, seeing it as no different than any other community organization. Often they struggle with time pressures from the world and confusing messages from a multitude of sources. Also, they have been turned away by what they perceive as boring worship services or by wounds inflicted in the past by someone in the church.

So why be involved in church? This very question was addressed by Paul concerning Titus's ministry in Crete. This island in the south of Greece was an old civilization with infamously low morals. Lacking capable leaders, the church there was filled with false doctrines taught by false teachers with false motives.

Titus was a seasoned leader sent by Paul to Crete to be a troubleshooter for this problem church. It was not an easy assignment. Why should he get involved? Why risk barriers, disappointment, and burnout?

Paul wrote to Titus to answer that question. He gave four reasons why building the church was worth the cost of involvement.

## I. THE CHURCH IS TO STAND FOR THE TRUTH.

**A.** The problem: In a secular society, truth is relative.

**B.** The Christian solution: In humility, take a stand for objective truth revealed in the Bible. Ultimate truth is in Jesus Christ (Ephesians 4:21) who is the way, the truth, and the life (John 14:6). Doctrinal truth was revealed by God in the Bible. We did not stumble upon it by ourselves.

**C.** The challenge: If the church does not stand for the truth of God against false teachings, who will?

## II. THE CHURCH IS TO STAND FOR MORAL VALUES.
**A.** The problem: The morality of Crete contrasted with Christian morality (1:12).

**B.** The solution: Ground morality in God.
1. His character is the moral standard of his universe.
2. Teach our vertical response to him as the basis for our horizontal response to fellow humans.
3. Godliness rather than a legalistic adherence to rules is the goal.

**C.** Challenge: If the church does not stand for God's moral values, who will?

## III. THE CHURCH IS TO STRENGTHEN THE HOME.
**A.** The problem: The families of church members seem to be as dysfunctional as non-church families.

**B.** The solution: Provide programs to help members, while modeling godly behavior in strong Christian families (Titus 2).

**C.** Challenge: If the church does not teach God's standard for the home, who will?

## IV. THE CHURCH IS TO EVANGELIZE THE WORLD.
**A.** The problem: People in Crete needed that which only conversion to Christ could give.

**B.** The solution: Paul sent Titus to Crete to carry out the Great Commission of Christ.

**C.** Challenge: If the church does not evangelize the world, who will?

## CONCLUSION
Why build the church? Because it is God's primary means of proclaiming his truth, teaching his moral values, strengthening Christian homes, and evangelizing the world. If the church does not do it, who will?

# Church Building
## (A Strong Congregation)

### *Titus 1*

Which gets the most attention in your church—survival or mission? A survival-driven church is concerned with management and maintenance. The goals of such a congregation include paying the bills, keeping attendance from declining, keeping the peace among members (even if it is a truce), and holding on to youth and young families. A mission-driven church is concerned with outreach and growth. This type of congregation pursues seeking and saving the lost and admonishing, teaching, and comforting brothers and sisters in Christ.

A survival-driven church is a monument, a slab of cold stone that at best hopes for erosion and decay to come slowly. A mission-driven church is a body, a living organism that desires to grow to maturity and reproduce abundantly. Our mission as the church is to be this body of Christ in the twentieth century.

Paul encourages Titus to reject the survival-driven mentality in the churches of Crete. This letter is a call to create mission-driven congregations. Merely maintaining Cretan congregations would be foolish. The congregations would survive but would continue to reflect an immoral culture, follow incapable leaders, remain in confusion over beliefs, exchange the gospel of grace for a religion of rules, and suffer fragmentation of church families.

The fact is, there will always be problems in the church. But confronting and addressing problems with a mission-driven attitude brings life and growth to a congregation. Paul gives three requirements of this type of church.

I. **TEACH THE TRUTH (THE ANSWERS TO THREE OF LIFE'S QUESTIONS—1:1-4).**
   A. The question of authority—Whom do I believe? Answer: You can believe Paul because of his credentials.
      1. His service shows him to be a servant of God in the great tradition of Moses and the prophets (1:1).
      2. His authority as an apostle was delegated from Christ himself on the Damascus road (1:1).
      3. His reliability is demonstrated in that God entrusted him with the proclamation of Christ's Word (1:3).

   B. The question of content—What do I believe? Answer: The Word of God is the basis of the faith "once for all entrusted to the saints" (Jude 3), the truth which is the very core of the gospel, and the hope of eternal life.

C. The question of behavior—What do we do about it? Answer: We must be godly, imitating the character of God **and** behaving according to the purpose of God.

## II. TRAIN CAPABLE LEADERS (1:5-9).

A. "Appoint elders"(1:5). Such men must be qualified by sound teaching, godly behavior, and willing hearts.

B. Standards for elders (wise leaders who shepherd by nurturing people and overseeing the work of the local congregation).
1. "Blameless" (1:6, 7)—This controlling standard in the list means to have no character flaw that brings reproach to oneself and the church.
2. "The husband of but one wife, a man whose children believe" (1:6)— The elder is responsible for two homes. Leadership in his own home is the chief testing ground for leadership in the church.

C. What an elder should not be: 1) self-willed, 2) quick-tempered, 3) addicted to wine, 4) violent in speech or action, 5) greedy.

D. What an elder should be (1:8, 9): 1) hospitable, 2) loves the good, 3) self-controlled, 4) upright, 5) holy, 6) disciplined, 7) hold firmly to the trust-worthy message, 8) encourage others by sound doctrine, 9) refute those opposing it.

## III. CORRECT FALSE TEACHERS AND FALSE TEACHING (1:10-16).

A. Correct with a spirit of humility. The goal is not to win the argument, but to win the people.

B. The behavior of a false teacher marks him. He is a rebel, an empty talker, a deceiver, an upsetter of families, and is out for dishonest gain.

C. How to tell false teaching:
1. It is a religion of rules (1:10).
2. It places traditions on the same plane as the gospel.
3. It expects the worst in people.
4. It opposes the truth. We must know the truth to discern the counterfeit.

## CONCLUSION

Strengthening the local congregation takes leaders that are truly disciples of Jesus. Such leaders are to teach and live the truth as Jesus did. They are to confront the things that keep people from God as Jesus did. Finally, these leaders are to be mission-driven like Jesus rather than maintenance-driven.

# Church Building
## (Strong Relationships)

### *Titus 2*

This sermon may be summarized in a simple statement. How we apply our faith to our relationships strengthens or weakens the church. That's because the world looks at the church to see if it really has what is missing in their lives.

There are four generations within the typical church. The congregation must work successfully with the gray wave, the boomers, the busters, and the youth if it is to strengthen its relationships within the body. These multiple generation gaps mean that interests, values, music, and needs are different. Members of each generation come to church as *consumers*, each with their own agendas. A congregation is successful when they become *contributors* to Christ's mission for the church. Only then do our relationships in the church "adorn" the gospel (2:10), making it attractive to the lost.

Into the pagan setting at Crete—proud, arrogant, self-sufficient, and sensual—Paul sent Titus to build the church. To permeate society with the gospel is our task and we do that primarily in the quality of our relationships. There are five sets of relationships in Titus 2 that impact the church.

## I. HOW SENIORS ARE TO RELATE (2:1-5)

**A.** Older men dispense wisdom (2:1, 2).
1. They have learned the gravity of life and self-mastery.
2. They are to be sober, sensible, serious, and sound.
3. The years have taught them faith, love, and perseverance by experience.

**B.** Older women dispense kindness (2:3-5).
1. They are to be reverent in their behavior (a word used to describe sacred things).
2. They are not to be gossips or addicted to wine.
3. They are to teach younger women in the church by words and conduct.
4. The purpose of all this is so the gospel will not be maligned (2:5).

## II. HOW YOUNG ADULTS ARE TO RELATE (2:4-6)

**A.** Younger women learn to nurture (2:4, 5).
1. They must concentrate on making a good home and being the glue that holds it together.
2. They must be self-controlled and pure.

**B.** Younger men must learn to control their strength and ambition (2:6).

## III. HOW TEACHERS AND PREACHERS ARE TO RELATE (2:7, 8)

**A.** Leaders set an example in how they apply truth to their work.

**B.** Leaders model integrity, seriousness, and sound speech.

**C.** Leaders live so that even the opposition can say nothing bad about us.

## IV. HOW THE CHRISTIAN WORKFORCE IS TO RELATE (2:9, 10)

**A.** Christians in the workforce adorn the gospel with their work ethic.

**B.** They work hard and are obedient, honest, respectful, and trustworthy.

## V. HOW BEHAVIOR RELATES TO BELIEF (2:11-15)

**A.** The Belief: We live between Christ's incarnation and his second coming—his first appearance of grace and his second appearance of glory. (The word "appearance" means something previously hidden but now revealed. Christ was present before he ever came to Bethlehem's stable and he is present now awaiting the second advent.)

**B.** The Behavior: We therefore say "no" to ungodliness and worldly passions, living upright, self-controlled, and godly lives.


## CONCLUSION

The best way to strengthen our relationships within the church is to strengthen our relationship with Christ. Christ gave himself to redeem us from our wickedness and to save us. He wants us for his very own special people. (The expression signifies the best spoils of battle set aside for the king's own possession.) We must not "spoil the spoils" by disqualifying ourselves. We can say "no" to Christ or we can say "yes" to him. The choice is ours for all eternity.

# Church Building
## (A Strong Witness)

### *Titus 3*

Simply put, as the church we are to walk the talk and talk the walk. We are to live out what we profess and we are to "gossip" the gospel. Both are necessary to strengthen our Christian witness to the world.

If Titus had lived a good moral life and taught the church on Crete to live morally, he would have won no one to Christ. On the other hand, if he had proclaimed the gospel and had lived a wicked life, his words would have been hollow.

There are two things God wants of the church in any community. Francis Schaeffer describes it as a church that preaches and teaches the gospel and lives it out before the eyes of a watching world. These two sides of witnessing are elaborated in this text.

## I. WE WITNESS BY OUR WALK (3:1-3).
**A.** We walk as  good citizens (3:1, 2).
1. We must be law abiding—the only way to avoid anarchy and chaos.
2. We must be active in service—both in the church and in the community (balanced).
3. We must be careful how we speak, maligning no one and practicing the Golden Rule.
4. We must be tolerant, not pugnacious.
5. We must be kind, not merely by the letter of the law, but from the heart.
6. We must be gentle, keeping our temper under control.

**B.** We avoid the old paths of life (3:3).
1. We once were foolish, disobedient, deceived, enslaved by lusts and pleasures.
2. The pattern of our lives was living in malice, envy, being hated and being hateful.
3. When people see the change that Christ has made in our lives, they will want what we have found.

## II. WE WITNESS BY OUR TALK (3:4-11).
**A.** We use talk that redeems (3:4-8).
1. We must talk about Bethlehem, because Jesus' birth demonstrated the kindness and love of God.

2. We must talk about Calvary because we are saved through Jesus' death on the cross. Salvation comes not by our merit or works but because of his mercy. He washed us and renewed us with the Holy Spirit. (Compare 3:5 with John 3:5 and Acts 2:38.)
3. We must talk about the new life he gives. We are justified by his grace. Justified is a legal term meaning God treats the guilty as not guilty because of what Christ did. Furthermore, we are made heirs. We inherit the hope of eternal life from our Father because his firstborn Son conquered death.
4. We must talk about our reasons for speaking as boldly as we do. We desire that "those who have trusted in God may be careful to devote themselves to doing what is good," knowing that "these things are excellent and profitable for everyone" (3:8).

**B.** We use talk that rebukes (3:9-11).
1. We must refuse to waste time on the wrong kinds of questions. We have no time for speculations, family trees, and arguing over petty rules.
2. We must not tolerate the wrong kind of attitude and behavior. Such behavior expresses itself in divisive language. When someone attempts to cause division, we must warn that person twice. Should he ignore our warnings, we must avoid association with such a person.

## CONCLUSION

The conclusion of the letter achieves the delicate balance of encouraging Titus to be both task-oriented and people-oriented. Titus is asked to join Paul as soon as he can. Furthermore, he is to assist Zenas and Apollos on their way and see that they have everything they need. He is to teach the church to do good in order to be productive and provide for daily necessities. Finally, he is to pass along Paul's greetings, not just Paul's commands. People are more important than programs.

# A Few Neglected Words
## (Greetings That Grip)
### 1 Timothy 1:1, 2;
### 2 Timothy 1:1, 2; Titus 1:1-4

Neglected words cause us problems. We must never forget to say, "Thank you," "I'm sorry," "I made a mistake," or "I love you." Likewise, we must never underestimate the importance of the first words and last words that we use in letters, sales presentations, teaching, speeches, or sermons. Strong openings and closings are crucial in clearly communicating our messages. We dare not neglect them.

We dilute the impact of the Pastoral Epistles when we neglect Paul's words of blessing with which he opens and closes his letters. He greets Timothy and Titus with "Grace" (the greatest of the Greek greetings) and "Peace" (the greatest of the Jewish greetings). When writing to young Timothy, he includes "Mercy," probably because his son in the faith was facing a tough situation. These three often neglected words set the tone for the letters and introduce everything in them.

We do well if we listen for the echoes of these words all through the Scriptures. When we do so we can hear something of what Timothy and Titus heard in the nuances of the words. Let us consider examples of this verbal trinity, grace, peace, and mercy, throughout God's Word.

## I. THESE WORDS PRESENT THREE DESCRIPTIONS OF GOD.
   **A.** God is a God of grace.
   1. His grace is generous. He gives us what we need yet do not deserve through the death and resurrection of Christ.
   2. His grace is universal. He is not willing that any should perish but that all peoples would come to repentance.
   3. His grace is powerful. It is greater than all the sin and evil in the world.
   4. To greet someone with "charis" (grace) is to bless them with God's life-sustaining grace.

   **B.** God is a God of peace.
   1. His gift of peace is more than the absence of conflict.
   2. It is the blessing of well-being in the fullest sense: contentment, safety, welfare, happiness, prosperity, and health.
   3. It is not dependent on good times. In fact, it often comes in the eye of the storm around us.
   4. To greet someone with "shalom" (peace) is to bless them with God's everlasting peace.

47

**C.** God is a God of mercy.
1. His mercy to us reveals his heart of compassion.
2. He forgives us our sins because he is merciful.
3. He helps us when we cannot help ourselves because of his mercy.
4. To greet someone with "eleos" (mercy) is to bless them with "May God be good to you."

## II. THESE WORDS ARE ILLUSTRATED BY THREE PARABLES OF JESUS.

**A.** God's grace is illustrated in the parable of the prodigal son (Luke 15:11-24).

**B.** God's peace is illustrated in the parables of the pearl of great price and the treasure hidden in the field (Matthew 13:44-46).

**C.** God's mercy is illustrated in the parable of the good Samaritan (Luke 10:25-37).

## III. THESE WORDS ARE THE THEMES OF THREE BEATITUDES FROM THE SERMON ON THE MOUNT.

**A.** Grace: "Blessed are the poor in spirit, for theirs (by grace) is the kingdom of heaven" (Matthew 5:3).

**B.** Peace: "Blessed are the peacemakers, for they will be called sons of God" (Matthew 5:9).

**C.** Mercy: "Blessed are the merciful, for they will be shown mercy" (Matthew 5:7).

## IV. THESE WORDS ARE SEEN IN THREE BEAUTIFUL METAPHORS IN SCRIPTURE.

**A.** God's throne is called a throne of grace (Hebrews 4:16).

**B.** The golden lid on the ark of the covenant on which sacrificial blood was sprinkled is called the mercy seat (Exodus 25:17-22).

**C.** The peace of God will do sentry duty around your hearts and minds in Christ Jesus (Philippians 4:7).

## CONCLUSION

The letters begin with grace, mercy, and peace, and they all end with the benediction: "Grace be with you all." Paul's letters begin with grace in the singular and end with grace in the plural. They were written to Timothy and Titus, but they were meant to be read by the whole church. And they have our name on them.

Now abides grace, mercy, and peace, but the greatest of these is grace, and his name is Jesus. And you find all three of them—grace, mercy, and peace—in him.

# Words You Can Count On
## (Five Trustworthy Sayings)

### *1 Timothy 1:15; 3:1; 4:9;*
### *2 Timothy 2:11; Titus 3:8*

This week I noticed the symbols at the top of my computer screen. Do you realize how many options we find there for emphasizing important text? We have bullets, asterisks, bold type, italics, capitals, larger fonts, color, and underlining, to name a few.

Paul finds another way to emphasize his points in the Pastorals. Into the letters of Timothy and Titus Paul inserts five "trustworthy sayings." Of course, everything in the letters is trustworthy, but these words that "deserve full acceptance" are special instructions, doctrinal statements, and summaries.

Each statement is terse and memorable, almost like a proverb, perhaps borrowed from a familiar hymn or doxology, and is given Paul's own strong apostolic endorsement.

I. **1 TIMOTHY 1:15 TELLS US THAT CHRIST SAVES SINNERS.— "CHRIST JESUS CAME INTO THE WORLD TO SAVE SINNERS— OF WHOM I AM THE WORST."**

   A. "Christ Jesus came into the world to save . . . " This was his purpose for coming. The historic ministry of Jesus is the basis of salvation. This ministry continues to be effective today through the preaching of the gospel.

   B. Paul called himself "the worst" of sinners. Paul's conversion is the perfect illustration of the effectiveness of the gospel and the boundless grace and patience of God.

II. **1 TIMOTHY 3:1 TELLS US THAT A GODLY ELDER DOES A GRAND WORK.—"IF ANYONE SETS HIS HEART ON BEING AN OVERSEER, HE DESIRES A NOBLE TASK."**

   A. Notice that the term "office" never appears in the text. Rather it is a task, a service, a function on which one sets his heart. The emphasis is on ministry, not on office or position.

   B. "Noble task" describes how both the overseers and the members are to see the work of an elder.

III. **1 TIMOTHY 4:8 TELLS US THAT SPIRITUAL DISCIPLINE IS INVALUABLE BOTH IN THIS LIFE AND THE NEXT.—"FOR**

PHYSICAL TRAINING IS OF SOME VALUE, BUT GODLINESS HAS VALUE FOR ALL THINGS, HOLDING PROMISE FOR BOTH THE PRESENT LIFE AND THE LIFE TO COME."

**A.** Physical exercise has limited value. It is temporary, limited to this life, and only forestalls the inevitable. Unless Jesus returns soon, we all are going to die. (These words are especially important in an age when we have made an idol out of physical exercise and sports.)

**B.** Godliness has unlimited value. Spiritual exercise blesses us in this life and in the life to come.

## IV. 2 TIMOTHY 2:11-13 TELLS US THAT HOW WE TREAT CHRIST DETERMINES OUR DESTINY:

"If we died with him,
we will also live with him;
If we endure,
we will also reign with him.
If we disown him,
he will also disown us;
If we are faithless,
he will remain faithful,
for he cannot disown himself."

## V. TITUS 3:8 TELLS US THAT OUR FAITH IN CHRIST DETERMINES HOW WE BEHAVE.—"STRESS THESE THINGS, SO THAT THOSE WHO HAVE TRUSTED IN GOD MAY BE CAREFUL TO DEVOTE THEMSELVES TO DOING WHAT IS GOOD." THIS VERSE HAS BEEN CALLED THE MOTIVE FOR CHRISTIAN LIVING IN THE WORLD. IT IS BASED ON WHAT GOD HAS DONE FOR US.

**A.** He came to earth because he loves us (3:4).

**B.** He saves us because of his mercy, not our merit (3:5). This salvation comes through the washing of rebirth (baptism) and through the renewal of the Holy Spirit (Acts 2:38).

**C.** He makes us heirs with the hope of eternal life (3:7).

**D.** He wants us to devote ourselves to doing good (3:1, 2, 8).

## CONCLUSION

Christ gave us these words we can trust. All five special sayings add emphasis to his message to Timothy, Titus, and the church at large. Can he trust us to obey these words?

# Praise God!
## (Doxologies to Timothy)
### *1 Timothy 1:17; 3:16; 6:15, 16; 2 Timothy 2:11-13*

What does a person have to sing about when he is in prison on a trumped-up charge and is facing imminent death? We learn the answer to that question in the doxologies that pour from his lips out of a thankful heart. Paul's doxologies and hymn fragments are peaks of praise jutting up from his plains of prose, and they give lyrical impact to his ideas.

He includes two doxologies and two hymn fragments in his letters to Timothy. The hymns would have been familiar to Timothy. The doxologies were either commonplace praises in the early church or they originated in the great heart of Paul.

It is almost criminal to attempt to dissect a doxology or a hymn, but there is value in underlining its key theme and learning to duplicate its praise. Listen to Paul's four melodies of the soul in his letters to Timothy.

I. **A SONG OF PRAISE TO GOD FOR SALVATION IN CHRIST THAT TRANSFORMS SINNERS—"NOW TO THE KING ETERNAL, IMMORTAL, INVISIBLE, THE ONLY GOD, BE HONOR AND GLORY FOR EVER AND EVER. AMEN" (1 TIMOTHY 1:17).**

   A. Paul brings honor and glory to God for being the great God he is.
      1. Paul praises God who is eternal—beyond the limits of time.
      2. Paul praises God who is immortal—beyond the limit of death and the grave.
      3. Paul praises God who is invisible—beyond every limit we can see.
      4. Paul praises God who is the only God—vastly beyond the limit of any competition for our allegiance.

   B. Paul praises God for using him as exhibit A to encourage others who are on the edge of accepting Jesus. Through his work with Paul God demonstrates what he can do to change lives. He still transforms sinners.

II. **A SONG OF PRAISE FOR THE LORD OF THE CHURCH WHO IS EQUALLY AT HOME IN THE EARTH AND HEAVEN—"BEYOND ALL QUESTION, THE MYSTERY OF GODLINESS IS GREAT: HE WHO APPEARED IN A BODY, WAS VINDICATED BY THE SPIRIT, WAS SEEN BY ANGELS, WAS PREACHED AMONG THE**

NATIONS,
WAS BELIEVED ON IN THE WORLD, WAS TAKEN UP IN
GLORY" (1 TIMOTHY 3:16).

A. If the God of Heaven has come to earth, we need to change our behavior.

B. Paul used this section of a hymn to summarize his treatise on Christian
behavior which he had been discussing in 2:1-3:15.

III. A SONG OF PRAISE FOR GOD'S SOVEREIGN MAJESTY AND
THE FAITHFUL OBEDIENCE DUE HIM—"GOD, THE BLESSED
AND ONLY RULER, THE KING OF KINGS AND LORD OF
LORDS; WHO ALONE IS IMMORTAL AND WHO LIVES IN
UNAPPROACHABLE LIGHT, WHOM NO ONE HAS SEEN OR
CAN SEE. TO HIM BE HONOR AND MIGHT FOREVER. AMEN "
(1 TIMOTHY 6:15, 16).

A. God's majesty and authority awesomely overshadows that of mortal man.

B. This doxology summarizes Paul's appeal to Timothy to be faithful to the
ministry until the coming of Christ (vv. 11-14).

IV. A SONG OF PRAISE FOR THE FAITHFULNESS OF THE LORD—
"HERE IS A TRUSTWORTHY SAYING:
IF WE DIED WITH HIM, WE WILL ALSO LIVE WITH HIM;
IF WE ENDURE, WE WILL ALSO REIGN WITH HIM;
IF WE DISOWN HIM, HE WILL ALSO DISOWN US;
IF WE ARE FAITHLESS, HE WILL REMAIN FAITHFUL, FOR
HE CANNOT DISOWN  HIMSELF" (2 TIMOTHY 2:11-13).

A. This song concludes the section urging us to fix our eyes on Jesus and to
remember his earthly ministry culminating in his resurrection.

B. The phrase, "descended from David," emphasizes his coming in the lineage
of King David as the messianic king, dying as a lamb for our sins, and raising
from the dead to conquer our greatest enemy: death.

## CONCLUSION

Praise and joy in the midst of suffering is a reoccurring theme in 1 and 2 Timothy.
Do not ever let anyone or anything take your hallelujah from you. We are not talking
about avoiding reality in dark situations. Christ gives songs in the night. He gave a
song to Paul and Silas at midnight in a Philippian jail. Their prayers and songs
brought on an earthquake that shook the jail so hard that it got the jailer's attention.
He heard the gospel gladly, and he and his household were baptized into Christ.
God not only gives us our hallelujah, he uses our praises to give his hallelujah to
others. What awesome power there is in praising the Lord.

# God's Photo Album
## (Part 1)

### *2 Timothy 4:9, 10*

The apostle Paul was the greatest missionary who ever lived except for Christ. One of his gifts was his magnetic ability to attract leaders to his cause—to stand them on their tiptoes with a fresh vision and to draw their best out of them.

Tucked away at the end of his second letter to Timothy are six verbal snapshots. This photo album displays glimpses of fellow workers who were extending the boundaries of the kingdom of God all over the Roman Empire. For the next two weeks we will thumb through these photos. We will look at each picture carefully and even turn them over to read the notes Paul left on the back. Today we will look at the first three.

### I. DEMAS—THE DESERTER

A. We can only guess at the specific reason he left.
   1. Paul says only that Demas "because he loved this world, has deserted me and has gone to Thessalonica" (4:10).
   2. Since the statement is general, it encourages us to fill in the blank with anything in our lives that causes us, like Demas, to love this world more than God.

B. Three invaluable things Demas lost:
   1. He lost the companionship of the great apostle Paul.
   2. He lost his opportunity to make his life count for eternity.
   3. He lost his soul unless he repented (and nowhere does the Bible say he did).

### II. CRESCENS—THE UNSUNG HERO

A. We know very little about Crescens.
   1. "Crescens has gone to Galatia" (4:10) is all that Paul tells Timothy.
   2. This is the only time his name is mentioned in the Bible.

B. Many others have served Christ faithfully but facelessly in Scripture.
   1. Of the twelve disciples of Christ, we know virtually nothing about James the son of Alphaeus and Thaddaeus. Matthias, who was chosen to replace Judas (Acts 1:23-26), received even less mention in Scripture. Yet we have no doubt that the gospel was spread throughout the Roman Empire

because of the efforts of these unsung heroes.
2. Ananias baptized Paul into Christ (Acts 9:10-19). Every time Paul preached the gospel, won a person to Christ, planted a church, or wrote a New Testament letter, Ananias received interest on his investment.
3. There are unnamed, unsung heroes in God's great roll call of the faithful in Hebrews 11. After his long list, the writer twice uses the term "others" and adds, "the world was not worthy of them" (v. 38).

C. Crescens represents all the unsung heroes in the church.
1. Many have served Christ faithfully over the past two millennia but were not in the limelight.
2. Many in this congregation serve Christ faithfully in often overlooked but vital jobs.

## III. TITUS—CHRIST'S COMMANDO

A. Titus was a seasoned troubleshooter in troubled churches.
1. He was sent to Corinth, a congregation struggling with division and carnality (2 Corinthians 7:13-16).
2. He was sent to Crete, a congregation filled with rebellion and deception (Titus 1:5, 10).
3. At this point, the church in Dalmatia must have needed his special attention.

B. His method was to preach and teach sound (healthy) doctrine. The doctrine was healthy and he presented it in a healthy way (Titus 1:9; 2:1).

C. Titus had hide thick enough to take it and thin enough to feel it.
1. Toughness and sensitivity combined is rare!
2. He understood Paul's teaching that false doctrine needed to be countered with both truth and love (Ephesians 4:14, 15).

## CONCLUSION

We are not called to an easy life. We may have the ministry of Crescens. We may labor hard for the cause of Christ, but get virtually no recognition. We may, on the other hand, get the recognition accorded to Titus. Because he had a reputation for successfully accomplishing difficult tasks, he was always given the "dirty jobs" in the church.

Either way, the results are better than those of Demas. No matter how hard the task we are given, we must not love the world and neglect our calling.

# God's Photo Album
## (Part 2)

### *2 Timothy 4:11, 12*

The body of Christ is composed of believers with different personalities, abilities, and callings. Tucked away in Paul's second letter to Timothy are six verbal snapshots of some fellow workers of Paul. Last time we looked at the first three of those: Demas the deserter, Crescens the unknown, and Titus the gospel commando. Today, let us look at the remaining three.

## I. LUKE—THE DOCTOR WITH TWO PRACTICES

**A.** The scholarship and attention to detail required of him as a doctor can be seen in the thorough research and the methodological presentation of the two books of the Bible he authored, Luke and Acts (Luke 1:3).

**B.** Likewise, all Christians need to look at their job skills and see how they can use their unique abilities to serve the Lord. As demonstrated by Luke, Christians are called to treat their profession or job as a focal point of Christian living and witness.

**C.** Luke understood that his primary calling was to be a Christian.
1. Luke traveled with Paul to Macedonia on his second missionary journey, traveled from there to Jerusalem with Paul at the end of the third missionary journey, and went and remained with Paul during his imprisonment in Rome.
2. Apparently Luke was a full-time missionary. There is no record that Luke practiced medicine on the mission field.
3. Like Luke, some are called to leave their professions or jobs and become full-time Christian leaders.

## II. MARK—THE BACKSLIDER WHO CAME BACK

**A.** Mark assisted Paul and Barnabas on their missionary journey (Acts 13:5).

**B.** He was with them at Cyprus but left at Pamphilia (Acts 13:13). We are not told the reason John Mark returned to Jerusalem.

**C.** Whatever Mark's reason, his leaving was seen as desertion and possibly betrayal by Paul.

1. When deciding to take a second missionary journey, Paul refused to take Mark with them (Acts 15:38).
2. The disagreement resulted in two capable teams of missionaries. Paul traveled with Silas and Barnabas traveled with Mark.

**D.** Years later Paul's assessment of Mark obviously changed. He told Timothy to bring Mark with him because "he is helpful to me in my ministry" (4:11).

**E.** We see here the great heart of Paul, the magnificent influence of Barnabas, and the grace of the God of the second chance.

## III. TYCHICUS—DEVOTED CHRISTIAN MESSENGER

**A.** Paul calls him "a dear brother, a faithful minister and fellow servant in the Lord" (Colossians 4:7).

**B.** This devoted friend had the gift of encouraging the church (Colossians 4:8)—a gift desperately needed in any age.

**C.** As God's mailman, he could be trusted to deliver the letters (the Word of God) faithfully to the churches in Ephesus and Colosse.

## CONCLUSION

From these brief snapshots, we see the remarkable diversity found in God's people. Do you see yourself in any of these small portraits?

Like Luke, do you allow your profession to be subservient to your faith? Or are you a John Mark, ministering today because someone was gracious enough to overlook youthful failures and give you a second chance? Perhaps you are Tychicus, gifted at encouraging others by supporting the ministry of others. There is a need for all types of servants in the Lord's church.

# Friends or Foes?
## (A Contrast Sermon)

### 1 & 2 Timothy 1:1; Titus 1:1

The pot of gold at the end of the rainbow has been found. It is a treasure beyond any other, and it has been given to us as a sacred trust to be kept secure during our lifetime and faithfully passed on to others as their inheritance.

Its name is the gospel of Christ, and it is precious beyond all the treasures of the world because it alone reveals how God puts a person right with himself through faith in Christ Jesus. Whether we are friends or foes of God depends on how we treat that message.

It will repay us to look in the Pastorals at some of the friends and some of the foes of the gospel to sharpen our understanding of what makes one either a friend of God or his enemy.

## I. CHARACTERISTICS OF THE FRIENDS OF GOD (ILLUSTRATED IN PAUL, TIMOTHY, AND TITUS)

**A.** All three share common characteristics.
  1. They teach us to love, respect, and trust each other in the way they served Christ together.
  2. They teach us to love Christ above all else and to demonstrate it with our godly lives.
  3. They teach us to love the gospel and to be committed to it because of what it has done for us and what we have seen it do in others.

**B.** They also have distinct individual characteristics.
  1. Paul was an archenemy of Christ who became an outstanding servant leader for him. His persecution of Christians made him the "worst of sinners" in his own estimation (1 Timothy 1:12-16). Yet he was called to be an apostle to the Gentiles on the Damascus Road and was converted to Christ (Acts 9:1-19). His zeal for evil was replaced by a zeal for good. If Paul can be saved and can serve, there is hope for everyone!
  2. Timothy was a young servant leader who allowed himself to be stretched for the sake of the gospel (1 Timothy 4:12).
  3. Titus was a seasoned servant leader who became an outstanding church troubleshooter for Christ. He was effective in resolving the difficult problems in the church in Corinth (2 Corinthians 7:6-14) and was sent to Crete to straighten out what was unfinished (Titus 1:5).

57

## II. CHARACTERISTICS OF THE FOES OF GOD

**A.** False teachers deceive.
1. Their false messages are sometimes blatant, sometimes peripheral, but always away from the gospel of Christ.
2. Their false methods tickled their listeners' ears by elaborate interpretations of obscure Bible passages that appealed to those seeking something new and different but did not challenge them to change their lives.
3. Their false motives were obvious in their thirst for money and acclaim.

**B.** Deceived believers desert.
1. The faith of Hymenaeus and Alexander was so shipwrecked that Paul gave them over to Satan to be taught not to blaspheme (1 Timothy 1:19, 20).
2. Phygelus and Hermogenes were leaders in the church who deserted Paul and what he stood for (2 Timothy 1:15).
3. Demas deserted Paul because he loved this present world (2 Timothy 4:10).

**C.** Those who reject Christ deny the power of God and attempt to destroy his servants.
1. For example, the Roman and Jewish leaders wanted Jesus crucified. The Romans crucified him because they thought he was trying to set up an earthly kingdom, and the Jewish leaders wanted him dead because they thought he was not.
2. Men and women will be godless in the last days (2 Timothy 3:1-9).
3. The godly will be persecuted (2 Timothy 3:12, 13).
4. Tradition claims that Paul was beheaded on the Appian Way outside Rome. His only crime was to proclaim Jesus as the only Savior and Lord.

## CONCLUSION

The living God is the one who eventually defeats all his foes. Are you his friend or foe? The evil one may do his worst to us, but like Paul, Timothy, and Titus, we trust God that he will rescue us from every evil attack and will bring us safely to his heavenly kingdom. "To him be glory for ever and ever. Amen" (2 Timothy 4:18). You can choose today to be a friend of God and that friend never fails.

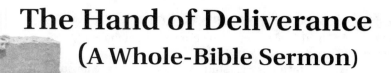

# The Hand of Deliverance
## (A Whole-Bible Sermon)

### *2 Timothy 3:10-17*

The idea for this sermon came from a diagram in a book of chart sermons edited by Z. T. Sweeney. In outlining the content of the entire Bible, it pictures a person's hand. Each finger and thumb represents a main heading of the outline. The hand has a pierced palm representing the death, burial, and resurrection of Christ.

This is one of my favorite outlines of the Bible. It provides a brief overview of the Scriptures and is Christ-centered. But best of all, it is totally *portable*. (It goes everywhere one's hand goes!)

While we worship the Lord, not the Bible, the Book is a necessity for our walk with him. In the words of Paul to Timothy, it is "God-breathed and is useful for teaching, rebuking, correcting and training in righteousness" (2 Timothy 3:16).

## I. COMING UP TO CHRIST—THE OLD TESTAMENT.

**A.** The Old Testament has an amazing diversity. Written over hundreds of years, it contains five books of Law, twelve books of history, five books of poetry, and seventeen books of prophecy.

**B.** But because of Christ there is also an amazing unity. The following are three examples:
1. Genesis 3:15 prophesied that the offspring of the woman would crush the serpent's head, and he would strike his heel. This prophecy came true at Calvary when Christ defeated Satan by dying on the cross for our sins.
2. Genesis 12:1-3 records the Lord's promise to Abraham that all peoples on earth shall be blessed through him. That promise was carried out in the rest of the Bible and culminated in the ministry of Christ.
3. Isaiah's description of the Suffering Servant in chapter 53 fits the sacrifice of Christ so perfectly that his book has been called "The Fifth Gospel."

## II. COMING OF CHRIST—THE FOUR GOSPELS.

**A.** Mark 10:45 summarizes the message of the four Gospels: "For even the Son of Man did not come to be served, but to serve, and to give his life as a ransom for many."

**B.** His life and teachings, his death, burial, and resurrection, and his now-and-future kingdom reveal God to us. Furthermore, he reveals his will for our lives and how we can have fellowship with him.

## III. COMING INTO CHRIST—ACTS.

A. The theme of Acts is the evangelism of the world (1:8).

B. Luke includes case studies of conversions to illustrate how the early church obeyed the Great Commission.
  1. 3,000 on Pentecost (Acts 2)
  2. Ethiopian Eunuch (Acts 8)
  3. Saul of Tarsus (Acts 9)
  4. Cornelius (Acts 10, 11)
  5. Lydia (Acts 16)
  6. Philippian Jailer (Acts 16)

C. When we respond as they did, we share their promise of salvation.

## IV. CONTINUING WITH CHRIST—THE LETTERS.

A. Fourteen letters were written to specific people or congregations to instruct them in their Christian life.

B. Seven letters were written to general readers to encourage them in their Christian life.

C. Attending to their message will keep us faithful to the end.

## V. CROWNED WITH CHRIST—REVELATION.

A summary of the message of Revelation: "Be faithful, even to the point of death, and I will give you the crown of life" (2:10).

## CONCLUSION

Two texts from the apostle John express the central message of the Bible:

1. "He who has the Son has life; he who does not have the Son of God does not have life" (1 John 5:12).

2. "For God so loved the world that he gave his one and only Son, that whoever believes in him shall not perish but have eternal life" (John 3:16).

# The Saga of a City Church
## (A Case Study)

*Acts 19; Ephesians; 1 & 2*
*Timothy; Revelation 2*

Before planting a new church, a church planter needs to do a feasibility study. Why did Paul, the most effective church planter of the first century, pick Ephesus?

Demographically, it was a Roman colony situated at the mouth of the Cayster River between the Koressos Mountain range and the Mediterranean Sea on the western side of Asia Minor. Like other Roman colonies it was located as a gateway to the trade and resources from the interior.

By New Testament times the great days of her trade were past because top soil from the stripped forests of the interior had washed down and nearly filled the harbor. So the city turned to tourism to bolster its economy. The magnificent Temple of Artemis, built by Alexander the Great, drew multitudes. The pagan worship of the cult featured Artemis, a nature-goddess associated with carnal fertility rites and prostitution. Of particular fame was a meteoric stone which the devotees claimed fell from Jupiter.

The building was four times the size of the Parthenon in Athens, and tradesmen and hucksters stationed around the shrine found a living by supplying visitors with food, lodging, dedicatory offerings, and silver souvenirs. The Temple was also a treasury and a private bank where individuals, kings, and cities made deposits.

Because of its prime location from which all Asia could be influenced, Paul committed himself to planting a strong church there. The following are some of the key chapters in the saga of this city church.

## I. THE CHURCH'S BEGINNING (EPHESUS IN ACTS 19)—PAUL HAD A STRATEGY FOR BIRTHING THIS CHURCH.

**A.** *Begin where people are.* Paul witnessed to and baptized 12 men who had known only the baptism of John the Baptist (vv. 1-7).

**B.** *Approach first those you know best.* He preached in the synagogue for three months until he was pressured to leave (v. 8).

**C.** *Use strategic, culturally appropriate ways to gain a hearing.* He held daily discussions in the lecture hall of Tyrannus for two years until "all the Jews and Greeks who lived in the province of Asia heard the word of the Lord" (vv. 9, 10).

**D.** *Bring forth fruits of repentance as a powerful testimony for the gospel.* He performed many miracles confirming his message, and many who owned books on sorcery burned them in a great bonfire (vv. 11-20).

E. *Allow God to make the wrath of men praise him.* Paul exited the city because of the riotous opposition to the church by the guild of silversmiths, but the church remained with many members (vv. 23-41).

## II. THE CHURCH'S MESSAGE (EPHESUS IN EPHESIANS)

A. In his book, *The Broken Wall,* Marcus Barth calls Ephesians the best commentary ever written on John 3:16.

B. The letter can be divided into two parts: chapters 1–3, God's design for the church; chapters 4–6, God's duty for the church.

## III. THE CHURCH'S STRUGGLES (EPHESUS IN 1 & 2 TIMOTHY)

A. Some members had gone after false doctrines and false teachers.

B. Church leaders needed to be carefully selected and trained.

C. The church needed to discipline heretical and ungodly members.

D. Both the rich and the poor needed instruction on the proper use of money.

E. Widows needed to be cared for properly.

F. Church leaders were urged to guard the sacred deposit of Christian doctrine entrusted to them.

## IV. THE CHURCH'S EVALUATION (EPHESUS IN REVELATION 2)

A. Christ commended them for their hard work, their testing and rejection of false teachers, and their suffering for the gospel.

B. Nevertheless, they had lost their first love.

C. In judgment they were told that unless they repented, the light of their congregation would no longer shine. Losing contact with Jesus, even when doctrine and practice are sound, causes the lamp stand to be removed. The congregation dies.

## CONCLUSION—THE CHURCH'S OUTCOME (EPHESUS TODAY)

There is no church there today. It died when the city died. Was it all for nothing? Absolutely not! For proof, think of your many Christian brothers and sisters won through Paul and Timothy's labors and those who faithfully passed on the sacred deposit of the gospel which was passed on to them. Meet them for the first time at the throne of God.

# Passing the Torch
## (A Sermon on Preaching)

### *2 Timothy 3:10–4:8*

The 1948 Olympic Games were held in England at Wembley Stadium before 80,000 fans with athletes from 60 countries competing. 1,700 young relay runners carried the Olympic torch from Mt. Olympus to Wembley, where the last runner touched the torch to the pedestal, causing the flame to burst forth and to burn throughout the games.

That Olympic relay is a parable of the Christian race: the runners are Christian leaders; the race is between the first and second appearances of Christ; and the torch is the flaming Word of God.

Our task is to carry it well and to pass it on to others who will carry it well and pass it on. This passage is a model for how to recruit, hone, and conserve capable Christian leaders. Look at four key ingredients.

## I. IMITATE GODLY MENTORS (3:10-13).

**A.** Imitate their ministry. Timothy knew Paul well because he observed him in ministry.

**B.** Imitate their lifestyle. Timothy knew all about Paul's way of life, purpose, faith, patience, love, and endurance.

**C.** Imitate their willingness to sacrifice to serve Christ. Timothy knew the persecutions Paul endured repeatedly for the gospel.

## II. INFORM YOURSELF WITH THE WORD OF GOD (3:14-17).

**A.** Know what it is ("God-breathed"—the meaning of "inspired").
   1. Timothy had two sources for knowing the Word of God: the Old Testament and the apostolic teachings of Paul.
   2. We have one rule of faith and practice: the whole Bible with both testaments. The Holy Scriptures referred to in this passage is the Old Testament because the New Testament canon was not yet formed, but what Paul said about the Old Testament applies supremely to the New.

**B.** Know what it does.
   1. It is able to make you wise for salvation through faith in Christ.
   2. It is able to equip you to become a mature Christian. It is useful for

teaching, rebuking, correcting, and training in righteousness. It can equip you thoroughly for every good work.

## III. IMPLEMENT WHAT YOU HAVE LEARNED (4:2).

**A.** Preach the Word. The living Word (Christ) revealed in the written Word (the Scriptures) must be heralded by the proclaimed Word (preaching).

**B.** Preach it with urgency. There has to be fire in the pulpit before there will be fire in the pew.

**C.** Preach it persistently, in season and out.

**D.** Apply it to the many issues that arise in the church.

**E.** Remember that the heart of our message is good news.

## IV. FOCUS ON POWERFUL INCENTIVES (4:3-8).

**A.** Be faithful because of the second coming of Christ and his certain judgment (4:8).

**B.** Be faithful because of the kind of world we live in. Both Timothy's world and ours cannot stand the truth.

**C.** Be faithful so that you can face death triumphantly. By living with Christian integrity, we can die with anticipation.

## CONCLUSION

The time will come for all of us when we must hand the torch to others as we leave the saints on earth and join the saints in Heaven. As soon as our hand releases the torch in death it will close around the crown of righteousness that God has prepared for those who love him.

Can we say with Paul, "I know whom I have believed, and am convinced that he is able to guard what I have entrusted to him for that day" (2 Timothy 1:12)?